Woman and Home

Microwave Cookery

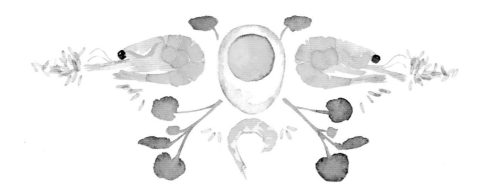

Woman and Home

MICROWAVE COOKERY

The Good Cook's Guide — over 200 recipes from the Woman and Home test kitchen

TREASURE PRESS

CONTENTS

The recipes in this book first appeared in
Woman and Home Microwave Cookery Nos. 1 and 2,
published by IPC Magazines Limited, 1985, 1986.

First published in this edition by

Treasure Press Ltd
Michelin House
81 Fulham Road
London SW3 6RB

Reprinted 1989

ISBN 1 85051 219 1

Produced by Mandarin Offset
Printed and bound in Hong Kong

Welcome to Woman and Home Microwave Cookery, a book of inspired recipes designed to help you make the very best use of your microwave oven.

'Magic' is a word that's often teamed with 'microwave', perhaps because when this method of cooking food first became widely available, it was greeted with some suspicion and surrounded in an aura of mystery. It was considered a trendy gadget by some, and to the unconvinced it seemed an expensive way of defrosting frozen dinners, melting chocolate or conjuring up a quick baked potato. How times have changed!

In the past few years we've learned a vast amount about the advantages of having a microwave oven in the kitchen, and not only in terms of its time- and energy-saving properties. We've learned, for example, that it cooks fish and vegetables beautifully, — and discovered the delights of a wonderfully light sponge pudding, produced in a matter of minutes. We've seen how well it can cook meat and poach fruit, and realised that excellent whole meals can be made with ease, for every occasion. Creative cooking in the microwave has come of age.

Woman and Home is noted for its high standards and the excellence of its cookery pages. From our Cookery Editor, Linda Collister, and her team come imaginative recipes that look good and taste marvellous. Alongside all the conventional cooking methods, we've been using and testing microwave ovens in the famous Woman and Home Test Kitchen for years, discovering what works in them – and what doesn't. Every time we've published microwave recipes in the magazine, requests have poured in for more. So we published a special microwave magazine, and then a second, and they were so popular that readers asked us to publish them as a book. This is the result.

All the original advantages of owning a microwave still hold good, of course – it's a great help for cooks who live alone, for couples who want a quick meal and for families with staggered mealtimes. There's the speed with which it can cope with small culinary jobs, the energy it saves (including yours), the washing up it cuts down on, its advantages for the freezer owner, and its sheer convenience. But there's more. Given some thought and imagination from the cook, the microwave can prove its versatility.

Creative cookery is no longer the province of the hob or conventional oven – our international recipes prove that. Try some popular Indian or Chinese dishes, spicy Mexican meals, or re-create memorable sun-drenched holidays with some favourite French or Italian recipes. And when you're entertaining, go for the gourmet touch. At Christmas, not only can you make all the traditional goodies but you can also rely on your microwave to make all the cooking so much less time-consuming. Pudding fanciers are not forgotten – there are treats galore for them – and because the microwave cooks vegetables so well, retaining their shape, colour, flavour and texture, meat-less meals are excellent. And there's no excuse for eating badly with our chapter on healthy eating!

Marvellous recipes, food that tastes terrific, plus a host of tips and hints – we hope this book helps you to value your microwave even more.

Sue Dobson
Editor

Prosciutto-Wrapped Mullet; Mango and Orange Oaty Crunch (p 10)

Single servings to please yourself

COOKING FOR ONE

When cooking for only one, it's easy to get into the habit of saying dismissively, 'It's just for me'. However, eating a home-cooked meal, even if alone, should be a pleasure, something to look forward to at the end of a busy day. Heating up a tin or packet of convenience food may be quick and easy, but it is not always nutritious or economical. But with the use of a microwave – plus a little imagination – you can eat delicious well-balanced meals without a lot of trouble and fuss. What's more, cooking one baked potato or one small casserole in a conventional oven is expensive and time consuming, while in a microwave it is both easier and energy-efficient.

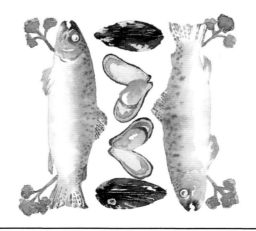

Prosciutto-Wrapped Mullet

1 medium red mullet, about 225 g (8 oz)
1 slice each onion and lemon
1 bay leaf
few sprigs of thyme
salt and pepper
2 teaspoons olive oil
25 g (1 oz) prosciutto, thinly sliced
2 tablespoons dry white wine

Preparation time: 15 minutes
Cooking time: 6–7 minutes
Microwave setting: High

Prosciutto, or Parma ham, can be thinly sliced for you at the delicatessen counter of supermarkets or specialist shops

—1—

Clean the mullet and rinse under a cold tap, scraping with the back of a knife to remove the scales. Trim the tail and fins. Pat dry on kitchen paper towels.

—2—

Fill the cavity with the slices of onion and lemon, and a few sprigs of thyme. Season lightly.

—3—

Brush the fish with oil and wrap in the ham. Put on to a plate and pour over the wine. If wished, add a little more thyme. Cover and microwave for 6–7 minutes until the fish is cooked through. Serve with salad.

Mango and Orange Oaty Crunch

½ small, ripe mango, peeled
½ small orange, peeled
2 tablespoons rolled oats
½ tablespoon demerara sugar
1 tablespoon plain flour
pinch each ground cinnamon and nutmeg
small knob of butter

Preparation time: 8 minutes
Cooking time: 2–3 minutes
Microwave setting: High

A hot, crunchy fruit crumble using juicy mango and other lovely, natural ingredients – a scrumptious, healthy "pud"

—1—

Cut the mango flesh into dice, and segment the orange, discarding the pith and any pips.

—2—

Put the prepared fruit into a large ramekin. Mix the oats with the sugar, flour and spices. Rub in the butter.

—3—

Sprinkle the mixture over the fruit. Microwave for 2–3 minutes until thoroughly heated. Serve with ice cream.

● Plan a menu for each day to ensure a well-balanced diet. Try to eat some fresh raw fruit or vegetables at each meal.
● Buy food "little and often" to ensure freshness. Avoid bargain offers of family-sized packs unless freezable.
● If you have a freezer, cook a recipe that serves four, then divide into individual servings, wrap and freeze.
● Use the correct-sized cooking equipment so food cooks evenly. Look out for attractive small-sized microwave- and freezer-proof casseroles and baking dishes.
● For a really quick meal, cook a large scrubbed jacket potato for 5 to 6 minutes in the microwave and serve with a favourite topping – cottage cheese, crispy bacon rashers, sour cream with chives, baked beans flavoured with chilli powder and cream cheese or smoked mackerel.

Halibut with Tarragon Cream Sauce

1 halibut cutlet, about 150 g (5 oz), rinsed and trimmed
3 tablespoons soured cream
3 tablespoons double cream
1 teaspoon fresh tarragon leaves
salt and pepper to taste
1 teaspoon olive oil
75 g (3 oz) green tagliatelle noodles
knob of butter

Preparation time:	10 minutes
Cooking time:	12–13 minutes plus standing
Microwave setting:	High

A meaty halibut cutlet (you could also use cod) is served on a bed of noodles and coated with a creamy sauce

— *1* —

Put the soured cream, double cream and tarragon in a small, shallow microwave-proof dish. Microwave for 2 minutes.

— *2* —

Stir the sauce then add the fish. Cover and microwave for 5 minutes or until the fish is just cooked. Season lightly and leave to stand, covered, while the noodles cook.

— *3* —

Put the olive oil into a bowl with 600 ml (1 pint) boiling water. Stir in the noodles. Microwave for 5–6 minutes until tender. Drain thoroughly then toss with the butter and seasoning.

— *4* —

Arrange the noodles on a warmed dinner plate. Top with the fish. Stir and season the sauce, pour over the fish and eat immediately.

Note: To make soured cream, add a teaspoon yogurt or lemon juice to 3 tablespoons double cream. Warm to blood heat, then leave to stand for 1–2 hours.

Nutty Stuffed Trout

1 medium-sized trout,
about 225 g (8 oz), cleaned
salt and pepper
15 g (½ oz) fresh wholemeal breadcrumbs
a few sprigs watercress
(leaves only required)
1 teaspoon olive or soya oil
1 tablespoon mayonnaise
1 teaspoon wholegrain mustard
1 teaspoon finely chopped onion
1 teaspoon grated lemon rind
15 g (½ oz) chopped toasted hazelnuts
To complete
1 tablespoon natural yogurt

Preparation time:	10 minutes
Cooking time:	6–8 minutes, plus standing
Microwave setting:	High

Hazelnuts, watercress and wholemeal breadcrumbs make a delicious and tasty filling for delicate trout

— *1* —

Rinse fish, trim tail and fins, and pat dry on kitchen paper towels. Lightly season the body cavity.

— *2* —

Mix the breadcrumbs with the watercress leaves, oil, mayonnaise, mustard, onion, lemon rind and nuts, to make the stuffing. Season lightly.

— *3* —

Spoon the mixture into the trout. Press the fish together to enclose the filling and secure with cocktail sticks. Place in a shallow baking dish. Cover. Microwave for 6–8 minutes. Leave to stand for 4 minutes – the fish should be thoroughly and evenly cooked and the flesh flake easily.

— *4* —

Remove the cocktail sticks. Spoon over the yogurt and serve with new potatoes and a green vegetable.

Garlic Stuffed Mussels

450 g (1 lb) fresh mussels
25 g (1 oz) butter or margarine
1 tablespoon chopped parsley
1 teaspoon lemon juice
1 clove garlic (or to taste), crushed
pepper to taste

Preparation time: 15 minutes
Cooking time: 8–9 minutes
Microwave setting: High

A generous helping of juicy mussels topped with a herb-rich garlic butter and served with lots of crusty French bread

—1—

Wash mussels in plenty of cold water. Scrape well and remove the beards. Discard any mussels that do not shut when tapped.

—2—

Put the cleaned mussels into a large bowl with four tablespoons of water. Cover with cling film and microwave for 5 minutes. Discard any mussels that have not opened.

—3—

Put the butter or margarine in a small bowl and cook to soften for 30 seconds. Beat in the parsley, lemon juice, garlic and pepper to taste.

—4—

Remove the top shell from each mussel. Arrange the lower shells, each containing a mussel, in a single layer on a large plate. Spread a little of the flavoured butter over each mussel.

—5—

Cover loosely with cling film and microwave for 2–4 minutes until the butter begins to sizzle. Serve immediately.

Poussin Stuffed and Roasted

1 poussin
knob of butter
1 small shallot, chopped
25 g (1 oz) fresh wholemeal breadcrumbs
½ tablespoon chopped fresh parsley
a pinch each dried marjoram and thyme
1 small carrot, peeled and grated
1 tablespoon chopped toasted hazelnuts
salt and pepper to taste
To complete
1 teaspoon lemon juice
small knob of butter
1 tablespoon chopped parsley

Preparation time: 5 minutes
Cooking time: 13–15 minutes
Microwave setting: High

—1—

Wipe the poussin inside and out with a damp cloth.

—2—

Put the knob of butter and shallot into a bowl and microwave for 2 minutes until softened.

—3—

Stir in the breadcrumbs, parsley, dried herbs, carrot, nuts and seasoning. When well mixed, spoon into the poussin (put any excess stuffing into a small dish and cook separately).

—4—

Put the poussin into a roasting bag and tie the ends with a rubber band. Microwave for 10–12 minutes until completely cooked and the poussin juices run clear. Leave to stand while making the sauce.

—5—

Pour the juices from the roasting bag into a bowl. Add the lemon juice and butter. Microwave for 1 minute, stirring after 30 seconds. Season to taste, then stir in the parsley and serve.

Salmon Steak with Herbed Butter Sauce

1 × 175 g (6 oz) salmon steak
For the sauce
1 shallot, very finely chopped
1 tablespoon white wine
salt and freshly ground black pepper
1 egg yolk
1 tablespoon lemon juice
25 g (1 oz) unsalted butter
1 tablespoon chopped fresh herbs

Preparation time: 5 minutes
Cooking time: 6–9 minutes
Microwave setting: High, then Low

Fish is excellent cooked by microwave, with the bonus of being so clean and easy. Choose as many or as few fresh herbs as you wish for the sauce – tarragon and chervil are our particular favourites

—*1*—

Put the salmon into a shallow dish with the shallot, wine and a little pepper. Cover with cling film and microwave on high power for 3–5 minutes, depending on thickness. Leave to stand for 2 minutes.

—*2*—

Put the egg yolk into a small bowl with the lemon juice and the juices from cooking the fish. Whisk until frothy.

—*3*—

Put the butter into a small bowl and microwave on high power for 45 seconds to 1 minute until melted. Gradually whisk into the egg mixture.

—*4*—

Stand the bowl in a shallow dish of hot water and microwave on low power for 2–3 minutes, stirring every minute, or until sauce thickens. Stir in the herbs and taste for seasoning. Pour over the fish and serve immediately.

Cherries Jubilee

110 g (4 oz) cherries
1 tablespoon sugar
The juice of 1 orange
1 teaspoon grated orange rind
1–2 tablespoons brandy or cherry brandy

Preparation time: 2–5 minutes
Cooking time: 4 minutes
Microwave setting: High

Traditionally served with vanilla ice cream, this luscious dessert can be made with fresh ripe cherries or canned cherries

—*1*—

Wipe fresh cherries, and stone if wished. Put the remaining ingredients into a serving bowl and microwave for 2 minutes.

—*2*—

Add the cherries and microwave for 2 minutes until thoroughly heated. Serve immediately.

Cherries Jubilee with ice cream; Salmon Steak with Herbed Butter Sauce

Cocktail of Mushrooms

75 g (3 oz) mushrooms, wiped
a small knob of butter or margarine
2 lettuce leaves, washed
For the dressing
1 tablespoon mayonnaise
1 tablespoon double cream or yogurt
½ teaspoon creamed horseradish
a dash each Worcestershire sauce and lemon
juice
salt and cayenne to taste

Preparation time: 10 minutes
Cooking time: 1–2 minutes, plus
standing
Microwave setting: High

This can be eaten as a first course or part of a salad since it is particularly good as an accompaniment for cold meats

—1—

Quarter the mushrooms into a bowl. Dot with the butter or margarine. Microwave for 1–2 minutes until just softened. Drain mushrooms and leave to cool.

—2—

Beat together the ingredients listed for the dressing and taste for seasoning. Fold in the mushrooms.

—3—

Arrange the lettuce leaves on a small plate and spoon over the mushrooms. If wished, sprinkle with a little paprika, strips of lemon rind or chopped parsley.

Beef Olive Italian-Style

1 × 100 g (4 oz) piece frying steak
1 thin slice Parma ham
2 spring onions, sliced
a small knob of butter
1 tablespoon fresh breadcrumbs
25 g (1 oz) mushrooms, chopped
1 teaspoon creamed horseradish sauce
salt and pepper
½ beef stock cube
1 tablespoon "Bon" (concentrated red wine for
cooking)
2 teaspoons plain flour
To garnish
spring onion curls

Preparation time: 15 minutes
Cooking time: 5 minutes
Microwave setting: High

An interesting and tasty way to eat steak. Serve with creamy potatoes and a salad

—1—

Put the steak between two pieces of cling film and beat with a rolling pin or meat hammer until very thin. Lay the Parma ham over the steak.

—2—

In a small bowl, cook the onions and a little of the butter for 1 minute until soft.

Mix in the breadcrumbs, mushrooms, horseradish and a little salt and pepper. Spread this mixture over the Parma ham. Fold in the sides and roll up neatly. Secure with cocktail sticks.

—3—

Dissolve the stock cube in 65 ml (2½ fl oz) boiling water. Stir in concentrated red wine. Put the beef into a small microwave-proof casserole dish. Pour in the liquid, then cover and microwave for 3 minutes.

—4—

Mash the remaining butter and the flour to a smooth paste. Add to the liquid around the meat, stirring gently until dissolved.

—5—

Microwave for 1–1½ minutes or until the sauce has thickened. Taste the seasoning then remove the cocktail sticks before serving. Garnish with spring onion curls.

Cranberry Glazed Chop

1 tablespoon cranberry jelly
small pinch ground nutmeg
½ tablespoon Worcestershire sauce
½ tablespoon chilli sauce (or a couple of drops of tabasco)
1 large lean pork loin or lamb chump chop

Preparation time:	5 minutes
Cooking time:	8 minutes
Microwave setting:	High

The tart, juicy flavour of cranberries goes equally well with lamb or pork

—1—

Put all the ingredients except for the chop in a small bowl. Microwave on high for 35 to 45 seconds.

—2—

Trim chop and remove excess fat. Place on a plate or shallow dish and microwave on high for 3 minutes. Brush with the glaze, cover loosely with cling film and microwave on high for 2 minutes. Stand for 2 minutes, then serve.

Chocolate Orange Mousse

Makes 2
50 g (2 oz) plain chocolate
1 teaspoon grated orange rind
1 teaspoon softened butter
1 egg, separated
4 tablespoons double cream
2 teaspoons finely chopped toasted hazelnuts
1 teaspoon orange liqueur or brandy (optional)

Preparation time:	10 minutes plus chilling
Cooking time:	1–1½ minutes
Microwave setting:	High

This heavenly recipe makes enough for two helpings – if you're strong-willed, invite a friend for supper or keep the second portion in the fridge for another meal

—1—

Break up the chocolate and put into a bowl with one tablespoon water. Cover and microwave for 1–1½ minutes until melted (do not overheat).

—2—

Beat in the orange rind, butter and egg yolk. Cool slightly.

—3—

Whisk the egg white until stiff then gently fold into the melted chocolate in two batches. When thoroughly blended, spoon the mousse into two glasses, ramekin dishes or small bowls. Chill for 2–3 hours until set.

—4—

Lightly whisk the cream until floppy. Stir in the hazelnuts and liqueur if using. Spoon over the mousses. Eat with crisp biscuits or shortbread fingers.

Tangy Zabaglione;
Sesame Chicken

Sesame Chicken with Noodles

1 teaspoon soft brown sugar
1 tablespoon soy sauce
1 tablespoon dry sherry
2 tablespoons wine vinegar
4 teaspoons sesame oil
pinch each of ground ginger
and garlic salt
black pepper and cayenne to taste
1 boned chicked breast
¼ teaspoon cornflour
¼ red pepper, shredded
2 spring onions, thinly sliced
50 g (2 oz) red cabbage, shredded
25 g (1 oz) walnut pieces
2 teaspoons chopped fresh parsley
75 g (3 oz) spinach noodles, cooked

Preparation time:	15 minutes plus chilling
Cooking time:	7–9 minutes plus standing
Microwave setting:	High

A colourful oriental-style dish that's quite quick to prepare

—1—

Combine the sugar, soy sauce, sherry and wine vinegar in a small bowl with two teaspoons of the sesame oil. Stir in the seasonings.

—2—

Cut the chicken into thin strips, stir into the marinade, cover and chill for 30 minutes.

—3—

Drain the chicken, reserving two tablespoons of the juices. Mix the reserved juices with the cornflour and coat the chicken in the mixture.

—4—

Place in a shallow dish, cover and microwave for 5–6 minutes, stirring halfway through the cooking time.

—5—

Stir in the red pepper and spring onions, recover and microwave for a further 2–3 minutes. Stir in the cabbage, walnuts, parsley and remaining sesame oil and leave to stand for 1 minute. Serve with hot noodles.

Tangy Zabaglione

3 tablespoons Grand Marnier
2 egg yolks
1 tablespoon caster sugar
1 teaspoon grated lemon rind

Preparation time:	10 minutes
Cooking time:	2½ minutes
Microwave setting:	High, then Low/ Defrost

Serve with pretty biscuits for a glorious, luxurious treat

—1—

Put the Grand Marnier into a small basin and microwave for 30 seconds.

—2—

Whisk together the egg yolks, sugar and lemon rind, then gradually whisk in the hot liqueur.

—3—

Microwave the mixture on low or defrost for 1 minute. Whisk well, then microwave on the same setting for 1 minute, whisking halfway through the cooking time.

—4—

Whisk gently then pour into an attractive glass and serve immediately with biscuits.

Oeuf en Cocotte aux Fines Herbes

15 g (½ oz) tiny fresh button mushrooms, wiped
a knob of butter or margarine
1 egg
salt
pepper
1 tablespoon chopped mixed herbs
1–2 tablespoons single cream

Preparation time:	5 minutes
Cooking time:	3 minutes
Microwave setting:	Medium

A delicious mixture of fresh herbs, cream, egg and tiny mushrooms in a ramekin

—1—

Put the mushrooms and butter or margarine into a ramekin. Microwave for 2 minutes.

—2—

Break the egg into the ramekin. Mix the seasonings with the herbs and cream and pour over the egg. Microwave for 1 minute. Serve as soon as possible.

Cod en Papillote

1 cod cutlet, about 225 g (8 oz)
a knob of butter
½ tablespoon cider
½ tablespoon double cream
salt and pepper
30 cm (12 in) square of greaseproof paper

Preparation time:	5 minutes
Cooking time:	8–10 minutes plus standing
Microwave setting:	High

This ancient cooking technique of wrapping food in an enclosing envelope to hold in the natural juices works especially well in the microwave

—1—

Wash the cod and pat dry on paper towels. Lightly butter the greaseproof paper.

—2—

Place the cutlet in the centre of the square of greaseproof. Turn up the edges slightly to capture the liquid then spoon over the cider, cream and seasonings. Dot with remaining butter.

—3—

Fold over the greaseproof paper and twist the ends to completely enclose the fish and cooking liquids. Lay the parcel on a plate and microwave for 8–10 minutes. Leave to stand for 4 minutes.

—4—

Open the cod parcel at the table to enjoy the full aroma. Serve with a baked potato and leeks in a creamy sauce.

● One of the great advantages of owning a microwave is that it enables you to be more adventurous in small quantities. ● For those who enjoy more adventurous cooking, we've included some special treat recipes for one, such as Prosciutto-Wrapped Mullet and there are many fuss-free dishes too.

Egg Benedict

1 thick slice bread or half a muffin
small knob of butter
1 medium-thick slice good quality lean ham
For the sauce
1 egg yolk
3 teaspoons lemon juice
salt and pepper
25 g (1 oz) unsalted butter, melted
1 tablespoon white wine vinegar
1 egg
chopped parsley to garnish (optional)

Preparation time:	5 minutes
Cooking time:	6 minutes
Microwave setting:	High, then Medium

Luxurious hollandaise sauce tops a very superior poached egg on toast

—1—

Toast the bread or muffin (remove crusts from bread first) and butter. Fold the ham to fit, then place on top of the bread.

—2—

Put the egg yolk, lemon juice and seasoning in a small bowl. Gradually whisk in the butter.

—3—

Stand the bowl in a shallow dish of water and microwave on high power for 2 minutes, stirring after 1 minute, until sauce thickens.

—4—

Put the vinegar and two tablespoons water in a ramekin. Microwave on high power for 45 seconds until boiling.

—5—

Break the egg into the ramekin and pierce the yolk with a cocktail stick. Microwave on medium power for 1 minute or until the white sets.
  Turn out and place on top of the ham. Spoon over the sauce and garnish with parsley. Serve immediately.

A Special Salad of Monkfish and Prawns

100 to 150 g (4–5 oz) piece monkfish fillet
25 to 50 g (1–2 oz) peeled prawns, thawed on paper towels if frozen
25 g (1 oz) button mushrooms
2–3 tablespoons mayonnaise
lemon juice, salt and pepper to taste
a few chopped chives
To serve
lemon wedges
a few crisp lettuce leaves (cos or iceberg)

Preparation time:	15 minutes plus chilling
Cooking time:	2–2½ minutes
Microwave setting:	High

The taste and texture of monkfish resembles lobster meat, and is just as delicious cold as it is hot. This recipe is enough for a main course for one or a starter for two people

—1—

Remove any white membrane surrounding the fish, then place in a dish, cover and microwave for 2–2½ minutes until the fish is opaque and just cooked. Leave to cool, reserving any fish juices.

—2—

Cut the cooled fish in bite-sized chunks and mix with the prawns. Wipe and trim the mushroom stalks.

—3—

Mix the mayonnaise with enough of the reserved fish liquid to make a light coating sauce. Add lemon juice and seasoning to taste. Fold in the fish, mushrooms and chives. Cover and chill. Stir gently then serve, garnished with lemon wedges, on a bed of lettuce leaves.

Cullen Skink

175 g (6 oz) smoked haddock
½ small onion, sliced
150 ml (¼ pint) milk
10 g (¼ oz) butter or margarine
150 g (5 oz) potato, peeled
2 teaspoons cornflour
salt and pepper to taste
1 tablespoon single cream or top milk
2 tablespoons chopped parsley

Preparation time: 20 minutes
Cooking time: 13–21 minutes
Microwave setting: High

A hearty soup, and no liquidizer is necessary – so you'll have little washing up to do afterwards!

—1—

Put fish and onion in a bowl with 3 tablespoons water. Microwave for 2–3 minutes or until the fish flakes easily. Carefully skin and bone the fish.

—2—

Roughly chop potato and put into a bowl of boiling salted water. Microwave for 5–7 minutes (or until soft). Drain and mash potatoes and put into microwave-proof bowl.

—3—

Microwave milk in jug for 2 minutes. Dice butter and stir into milk. Add to potato and mix well. Microwave for 3–5 minutes; stir.

—4—

Blend cornflour with a little water and stir into potato mix. Cover and microwave for 3–4 minutes. Season to taste; stir in flaked fish and cream. Serve hot sprinkled with parsley. Accompanied by a chunky wholemeal roll, it will make a satisfying meal in itself.

Savoury Chicken Risotto

1 tablespoon soya oil
1 shallot or 2 spring onions, finely chopped
1 rasher streaky bacon, chopped
¼ green pepper, cored and chopped
50 g (2 oz) long grain rice
150 ml (¼ pint) boiling chicken stock
salt and pepper to taste
100 g (4 oz) smoked chicken, skinned
1 tablespoon sweetcorn
chopped fresh parsley to garnish

Preparation time: 10 minutes
Cooking time: 15–17 minutes
Microwave setting: High

Deliciously flavoured smoked chicken can be bought from delicatessens

—1—

Put the oil into a bowl with the shallot, bacon and green pepper. Cover and microwave for 5 minutes.

—2—

Stir in the rice and the stock. Cover and microwave for 8–10 minutes or until the rice is cooked.

—3—

Shred the chicken into bite-sized pieces and stir in with the sweetcorn. Cover and microwave for 2 minutes.

—4—

Stir then adjust for seasoning. Stir in parsley and serve immediately.

● How to make cream when you've run out, and the shops are all shut: Pour 115 ml (4 fl oz) full cream milk into a jug. Stir in 85 g (3 oz) unsalted butter cut into cubes. Microwave on high for 2 to 3 minutes to melt the butter. Liquidize the mixture and chill for a couple of hours.

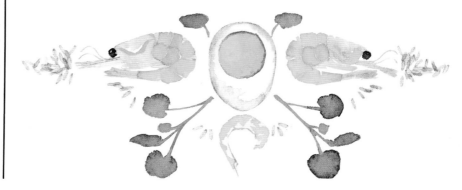

Cheese and Watercress Salad; Glazed Turkey Chops; Loganberry Claret Jelly; Spicy Avocado Dip (pp 22–23)

Recipes high in the good things of life

HEALTHY EATING

In the last few years we have all been made to realise that the food we eat affects our health and well-being in every way. The medical profession tells us that we should try to eat more fruit and vegetables, pasta, rice and pulses, and cut down on fats, sugar and salt. The microwave, together with our imaginative recipes, will help you to cook with the minimum of these 'less healthy' ingredients. And remember that the microwave excels at cooking vegetables perfectly, preserving the maximum of vitamins and minerals. In fact, cooking with the microwave leaves you with no excuse not to be healthy.

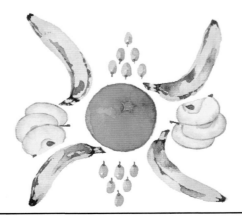

Spicy Avocado Dip

Serves 4
100 g (4 oz) low fat cream
cheese or soft cheese
1 medium tomato, skinned,
seeded and chopped
1 small onion, very finely chopped
1 large ripe avocado, peeled
3 tablespoons lemon juice
1 green chilli, seeded and very finely
chopped (optional)
salt, pepper and cayenne to taste
To serve
a selection of sliced raw vegetables

Preparation time:	10 minutes plus chilling
Cooking time:	2 minutes 15 seconds
Microwave setting:	High

A superb summer starter, or appetiser to serve with drinks before a special meal

—1—

Put the cream/soft cheese into a bowl and microwave for 15 seconds. Beat until very smooth.

—2—

Put the tomato and onion in another bowl and microwave for 2 minutes until softened. Cool, then mash until smooth.

—3—

Mash the stoned avocado with the lemon juice. Stir in the cheese, the tomato mixture and chilli, then season to taste.

—4—

Spoon into a serving bowl and chill until ready to serve, then surround with the prepared vegetables.

Cheese and Watercress Salad

Serves 4 to 6
2 large bunches watercress
50 g (2 oz) walnut pieces
100 g (4 oz) low fat Cheddar-style cheese
2 crisp eating apples, washed
2 tablespoons lemon juice
For the dressing ·
150 ml (¼ pint) low fat yogurt
ground pepper to taste
5 cm (2 in) piece of cucumber, grated
1 clove garlic, crushed (optional)
2 tablespoons chopped mixed herbs

Preparation time: 10 minutes

This salad is lovely with baked jacket potatoes and glazed turkey chops (see page 23)

—1—

Rinse and pick over the watercress. Dry, then pick off the leaves. Put into a salad bowl with the walnut pieces.

—2—

Dice the cheese and add to the bowl. Quarter and core the apples, but don't peel. Cut into chunks and toss in the lemon juice. Add to the salad and toss gently.

—3—

Put all the ingredients listed for the dressing into a screw-topped jar and shake until blended. Pour over the salad and toss until well mixed. Serve immediately.

If you want to cut down on fats, sugar and salt:
● Cut down on butter and margarine as a spread and in cakes and pastries.
● Try not to eat more than four eggs a week.
● Use lean meat, with all the visible fat cut off.

● Fry less often – grill, poach, bake or casserole instead.
● Cut down on full-fat milk and cream. Try skimmed or semi-skimmed milk, and use yogurt instead of cream.
● If you are concerned about salt, reduce your consumption of

processed meats such as the types found in pies and sausages.
● Choose fruit canned in natural juice rather than sugar syrup. Choose low-sugar or sugar-reduced items such as jam and pure fruit spreads made without added sugar.

Glazed Turkey Chops

Serves 4
4 turkey breast chops (or 8
turkey leg chops)
For the marinade
1 small onion, chopped
1 clove garlic, crushed
few drops tabasco
1 tablespoon dark soy sauce
juice of 1 lime
2 tablespoons thick-cut, low
sugar marmalade

Preparation time:	5 minutes plus
	marinating
Cooking time:	7–8 minutes
Microwave setting:	High

Lean turkey breast chops are ideal for low-fat and low-calorie diets. This is an easy, tasty and economical recipe

—1—

Pat chops dry and arrange in a single layer in a shallow glass or china dish.

—2—

Put all the remaining ingredients for the marinade into a blender or processor and whizz until smooth. Pour over the chops and leave to marinate for 1–2 hours, turning occasionally.

—3—

Put the chops on to the microwave rack or a ridged microwave-proof dish. Microwave for 7 to 8 minutes until tender.

—4—

Garnish with a twist of lime, if wished, and serve with a mixed salad and baked jacket potatoes.

Loganberry Claret Jelly

Serves 4 to 6
450 g (1 lb) fresh or frozen
loganberries or raspberries
300 ml (½ pint) claret
caster sugar to taste
grated rind and juice
of ½ orange
4 teaspoons powdered gelatine
To serve
Greek-style yogurt
thin biscuits

Preparation time:	10 minutes plus
	chilling
Cooking time:	1 minute 15 seconds
Microwave setting:	High

Longanberries or raspberries combine with claret to make a simple, sophisticated dessert

—1—

Put the fruit in a bowl with two tablespoons water. Cover and microwave for 30 seconds (allow more time for frozen fruit). Sieve the fruit to remove the seeds, then make the purée up to 600 ml (1 pint) with water. Stir in the claret and sugar to taste, followed by the orange rind.

—2—

Put three tablespoons of the liquid into a small bowl with the orange juice. Sprinkle over the gelatine. Leave to soak for 5 minutes, then microwave for 45 seconds until the gelatine has melted.

—3—

Stir into the fruit liquid. When thoroughly blended pour into individual glasses and chill until set. Serve with Greek-style yogurt and elegantly thin biscuits.

King Prawns in Spicy Sauce

Serves 4

450 g (1 lb) Mediterranean king prawns
2 tablespoons oil
1 shallot, finely chopped
2 tablespoons chopped fresh
coriander or mint
2 cloves garlic, crushed
1 teaspoon each ground cumin and turmeric
3 tomatoes, peeled, seeded and diced
1 teaspoon tomato purée
salt to taste
1½ teaspoons garam masala
lemon juice to taste

Preparation time:	20 minutes
Cooking time:	10–12 minutes
Microwave setting:	High

King Prawns are a real treat cooked in this exotic curried sauce. Serve with fluffy rice, with a little wild rice if liked

—1—

Remove the heads and shells from the prawns but leave on the very ends of the tails. Wash, clean, and remove the black intestinal cord that runs along the back. Pat the prawns dry on kitchen paper.

—2—

Put the oil, shallot, garlic and coriander in a bowl. Cover with cling film and microwave for 2 minutes. Stir in the spices and microwave for a further 2 minutes.

—3—

Mix in the tomatoes, purée, salt and garam masala. Microwave for 3–4 minutes, until thick and pulpy.

—4—

Add lemon juice and prawns. Microwave for 3–4 minutes until piping hot.

King Prawns in Spicy Sauce

Risotto

Serves 3 to 4
225 g (8 oz) Jordans' Country Rice and Grains
2 tablespoons soya oil
1 large onion, finely chopped
2 cloves garlic, crushed (optional)
1 red pepper, cored and diced
600 ml (1 pint) boiling chicken or vegetable stock
225 g (8 oz) cooked boneless chicken meat, shredded
100 g (4 oz) button or oyster mushrooms, quartered
salt and pepper to taste
To complete
2 tablespoons watercress leaves
2 tablespoons grated Parmesan cheese

Preparation time:	25 minutes plus soaking
Cooking time:	28–34 minutes plus standing
Microwave setting:	High

Jordans' Country Rice and Grains is a tasty mix of brown rice and five other whole-grains. It is sold in health food shops

—1—

Cover the Rice and Grains with cold water. Leave to soak for 5 minutes, then drain. Meanwhile, put the oil into a large bowl. Microwave for 40 seconds.

—2—

Stir in the onion, garlic and red pepper. Cover and microwave for 2–4 minutes until softened.

—3—

Stir in the drained grain mixture and the boiling stock. Cover and microwave for 20–25 minutes, stirring every 5 minutes, until just cooked.

—4—

Stir in the chicken and mushrooms and season to taste. Microwave for 5 minutes. Leave to stand for 5 minutes. Stir in the watercress and Parmesan and serve immediately.

Eggs Florentine

Serves 1 for supper, or 2 as a starter
225 g (8 oz) frozen leaf spinach
salt, pepper and nutmeg
2 eggs
3 tablespoons single cream or top of the milk
2 tablespoons Gruyère or Cheddar cheese, grated
2 teaspoons dry white breadcrumbs

Preparation time:	10 minutes
Cooking time:	5 minutes, plus standing
Microwave setting:	High

Use your microwave to prepare this classic dish in minutes

—1—

Microwave the spinach as directed on the packet. Drain well, pressing to extract all the moisture. Season with salt, pepper and nutmeg. Spoon into a microwave-proof shallow dish.

—2—

Make two hollows in the spinach with the back of a spoon and break an egg into each. Prick the yolks. Cover dish with pierced cling film and microwave for 2 minutes. Leave to stand, covered for 1 minute, until the yolks are set.

—3—

Stir the cream and grated cheese together and spoon over the eggs. Sprinkle with breadcrumbs and brown quickly under a hot grill. Serve immediately.

Summer Chicken

Serves 4

1 medium onion, thinly sliced
1 clove garlic, crushed
1 teaspoon soya oil
4 chicken supremes (boneless
chicken breasts)
50 ml (2 fl oz) chicken stock
85 ml (3 fl oz) dry white wine
juice of ½ lemon
salt and pepper
5 cm (2 in) piece of cucumber, skinned
175 g (6 oz) tomatoes, skinned, seeded and
quartered
chopped parsley to garnish

Preparation time:	20 minutes
Cooking time:	22–25 minutes
Microwave setting:	High and conventional hob

Place the onion and garlic in a microwave-proof dish, cover and microwave for 4 minutes until softened.

Heat the oil in a non-stick frying pan on top of the stove and quickly fry the chicken supremes on both sides, until lightly browned. Drain, then add to the onion.

—3—

Pour over the chicken stock, wine, lemon juice and seasoning. Cover and microwave for 8–10 minutes or until the chicken is cooked through.

Remove the chicken supremes and place on a warmed serving dish. Reduce the cooking liquor by microwaving for 4 minutes.

—5—

Cut the cucumber into thin strips and add to the chicken juices with the tomato quarters. Microwave for 2 minutes. Spoon the sauce over the chicken and garnish with the chopped parsley. Serve with plain rice and a crisp salad.

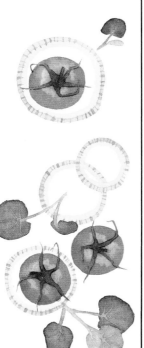

Brown Rice Pilau

Serves 4

100 g (4 oz) chicken livers, halved
1 tablespoon soya oil
25 g (1 oz) butter or margarine
175 g (6 oz) brown rice, washed
25 g (1 oz) toasted cashew
nuts, roughly chopped
25 g (1 oz) roasted peanuts
450 ml (¾ pint) boiling chicken stock
salt, pepper and soy sauce to taste
½ small red pepper, cored and diced
½ small green pepper, cored and diced

Preparation time:	15 minutes
Cooking time:	17–20 minutes plus standing
Microwave setting:	High

The chicken livers can be replaced with diced cooked chicken or fish, if wished

—1—

Put the livers into a bowl with the oil. Cover and microwave for 1–2 minutes, stirring occasionally.

—2—

Put the butter into a microwave-proof casserole. Microwave for 30 seconds or until melted.

—3—

Stir in the rice, and microwave for 1 minute. Stir in the nuts. Microwave for 2 minutes.

—4—

Add the remaining ingredients, including the livers, and stir well. Cover and microwave for 13–15 minutes until the rice is just tender, stirring twice during the cooking.

—5—

Leave to stand for 4–5 minutes, then stir gently, taste for seasoning and serve.

Variation
For a milder flavour, soak the livers in a little milk for 1–2 hours before cooking.

Pasta with Seafood in Tomato Sauce

Serves 4

450 g (1 lb) mussels or clams
or 225 g (8 oz) shelled mussels
2 tablespoons soya oil
2 cloves garlic, crushed
1 small onion, chopped
450 g (1 lb) tomatoes, skinned and chopped
2 tablespoons tomato purée
6 tablespoons white wine,
vermouth or water
4 tablespoons chopped fresh parsley
½ teaspoon dried thyme
salt, pepper and tabasco sauce to taste
225 g (8 oz) shelled prawns
350 g (12 oz) spaghetti

Preparation time:	15 minutes
Cooking time:	27–36 minutes plus standing
Microwave setting:	High

—1—

Scrub the mussels or clams well, removing any 'beards' or barnacles with a sharp knife, and discarding any that remain open when tapped.

—2—

Put the oil, garlic and onion into a large bowl, cover and microwave for 2–3 minutes. Add the tomatoes, purée, wine, parsley, thyme and a very little seasoning. Microwave for 10–12 minutes uncovered, stirring during the cooking time.

—3—

Stir in the mussels or clams. Cover and microwave for 5 minutes. Stir well and discard any mussels or clams that haven't opened. Add the prawns and microwave for 2–4 minutes. Cover and leave to stand for 5 minutes. Taste for seasoning.

—4—

Cook the pasta in a bowl of boiling water for 8–12 minutes until tender (or cook on top of the cooker). Drain well and put into a warmed serving dish. Spoon over the sauce and serve immediately.

Poisson Julienne

Serves 5 to 6
For the sauce
1 medium onion, finely chopped
25 g (1 oz) butter or margarine
450 g (1 lb) carrots
1 wineglass white wine
1 level teaspoon plain flour
150 ml (¼ pint) fish stock
a bay leaf and a sprig of thyme
salt and pepper to taste
For the fish
750 g (1½ lb) monkfish
50 g (2 oz) seasoned flour
25 g (1 oz) butter
1 tablespoon oil
chopped parsley

Preparation time:	20 minutes
Cooking time:	15–17 minutes plus standing
Microwave setting:	High

Colourful, with a deliciously piquant flavour, this dish is surprisingly economical

—1—

To make the sauce, put the onion and butter in a bowl. Microwave for 2 minutes until soft. Peel the carrots and grate them coarsely, either through a processor or grater. Add to the onion with the wine, flour, stock, herbs and seasoning. Microwave for 6–8 minutes, stirring every 2 minutes.

—2—

Cut the fish into 5 cm (2 in) pieces and toss thoroughly in the seasoned flour. Put the butter and oil in a gratin dish. Microwave for 1 minute. Add the fish and toss to thoroughly coat in fat.

—3—

Microwave for 3 minutes. Spoon over the sauce. Microwave for 3 minutes. Leave to stand for a further 3 minutes. Sprinkle with chopped parsley and serve with new potatoes.

If you want to increase the fibre in your diet:
● Switch to wholemeal bread, and use wholemeal flour rather than white.
● Try brown rice - it has a deliciously "nutty" flavour and it's ideal for those on low-calorie diets.
● Choose high-fibre pasta.
● Use more peas, beans and lentils in cooking; they're economical and tasty.

Filled Cheesy Potatoes

Filled Cheesy Potatoes

Serves 4
4 large jacket potatoes,
scrubbed
sea salt
For the fillings
(each fills 4 potatoes)
Filling 1
4 rashers rindless bacon
(back or streaky)
4 slices Cheddar cheese
Filling 2
2 tablespoons chutney
½ onion, finely chopped
4 slices Cheddar cheese
Filling 3
½ onion, finely chopped
50 g (2 oz) tinned kidney
beans, drained
1 tablespoon tomato ketchup
100 g (4 oz) Cheddar
cheese, grated

Preparation time: 5 minutes
Cooking time: 25–32 minutes
Microwave setting: High

—1—

Dry the potatoes, then sprinkle with a little salt, if wished. Cut quite a deep cross on the top of each potato.

—2—

Stand the potatoes on the microwave turntable or shelf. Microwave for 20–25 minutes until tender.

—3—

Using oven gloves, squeeze each potato gently so the inside of the cooked potato is pushed up slightly.

For filling 1
Put the bacon on a ribbed dish or bacon rack or between two pieces of kitchen paper. Microwave until crispy, 4–5 minutes. Snip into pieces and divide between the potatoes. Top each potato with a slice of cheese. Microwave for 2 minutes, or until the cheese melts.

For filling 2
Divide the onion and chutney between the potatoes, then top with cheese and cook as above.

For filling 3
In a small bowl, mix the onion, beans, tomato ketchup and ½ tablespoon water. Microwave for 3 minutes. Spoon into the potatoes. Top with the grated cheese and cook as above.

Spicy Rice Pilaff

1 tablespoon soya oil
1 shallot, finely chopped
¼ teaspoon turmeric
a pinch of garam masala
¼ green pepper, cored and chopped
50 g (2 oz) long grain rice
150 ml (¼ pint) boiling chicken
or vegetable stock
salt and pepper
1 tablespoon toasted flaked
almonds (optional)

Preparation time: 5 minutes
Cooking time: 10–13 minutes plus
standing
Microwave setting: High

A useful rice dish to serve with grilled or roast fish, poultry and meat

Put the oil into a medium-sized bowl with the shallot, turmeric, garam masala and green pepper. Cover and microwave for 2 to 3 minutes, until the pepper is softened.

Stir in the rice, stock and seasoning. Cover and microwave for 8–10 minutes, or until the rice is just cooked.

Leave to stand for 2 minutes. Scatter with the almonds, if desired, and serve.

Redcurrant Fruit Spread

Makes two 350 g (12 oz) jars
450 g (1 lb) frozen redcurrants
25 g (1 oz) caster sugar, or to taste
3 teaspoons gelatine powder

Preparation time:	15 minutes plus setting
Cooking time:	11–13 minutes
Microwave setting:	Defrost, then High

This low-sugar spread can be served with savoury or sweet dishes. Store in the fridge

—*1*—

Put the redcurrants in a large bowl and microwave on defrost for 4 minutes.

—*2*—

Add four tablespoons water and the sugar, then microwave on high power for 6–8 minutes or until the fruit is tender.

—*3*—

Purée in a processor or blender, then sieve to remove seeds.

—*4*—

Sprinkle the gelatine over two tablespoons water in a small bowl. Leave to soak for 3 minutes then microwave on high power for 45–60 seconds until the gelatine has melted. Stir into the fruit purée. When well mixed, pour into warm, sterilized jars, cover and leave to set. Store in the fridge and use within three weeks.

Fresh Fruit Kebabs

a selection of fresh fruit such as apple, pineapple chunks, banana, strawberry, kiwi, mango
For the glaze
½ teaspoon cornflour
juice of ½ orange
1 teaspoon honey
1 teaspoon Drambuie, brandy or orange liqueur
2 wooden skewers

Preparation time:	15 minutes
Cooking time:	2 minutes
Microwave setting:	High

A pretty, and pretty easy, dessert to go with ice cream. A 'fresh' way to eat fruit, and to give yourself a treat

—*1*—

Prepare the fruit, peeling, coring and cutting into even-sized chunks as necessary.

—*2*—

Put all the ingredients for the glaze into a ramekin and microwave for 1 minute, stirring after 30 seconds.

—*3*—

Thread the fruit on to the skewers and lay on a plate. Brush thoroughly with the glaze and microwave for 1 minute. Serve the kebabs immediately.

Mixed Vegetable Soup

Serves 6
2 medium onions, peeled
3 small (or 2 medium) leeks, washed and trimmed
1 small turnip, peeled
1 medium potato (about 175 g/6 oz), peeled
1 stick celery, washed
1.2 litres (2 pints) boiling vegetable or chicken stock
50 g (2 oz) fresh or frozen spinach leaves
a bunch of watercress
200 g (7 oz) peas
200 g (7 oz) fresh or frozen broad beans
salt and pepper to taste
To serve
50 ml (2 fl oz) yogurt
1 tablespoon chopped parsley

Preparation time:	20 minutes plus cooling
Cooking time:	18–23 minutes
Microwave setting:	High

—1—

Finely chop the onions, leeks, turnip, potato and celery. Mix together in a large bowl. Cover and microwave for 3 minutes.

—2—

Pour on the hot stock and stir well. Cover and microwave for 7–10 minutes, stirring every 2 minutes.

—3—

Rinse and pick over the spinach and watercress, then shred. Stir into the vegetable mixture with the peas and broad beans. Cover and microwave for 7–8 minutes, stirring every 2 minutes, until all the vegetables are tender.

—4—

Cool slightly, then liquidize. Taste for seasoning and reheat the soup for 1–2 minutes until piping hot. Swirl in the yogurt and sprinkle with parsley before serving.

Midsummer Monkfish

Serves 4
450 g (1 lb) monkfish
1 tablespoon soya oil
½ small onion, finely chopped
100 g (4 oz) mangetout, topped and tailed
50 g (2 oz) broccoli florets
½ red pepper, cored and thinly sliced
100 g (4 oz) baby corn
2 tablespoons dry sherry
1 tablespoon light soy sauce
1 teaspoon cornflour

Preparation time:	15 minutes
Cooking time:	12 minutes
Microwave setting:	High

Monkfish is a lovely 'meaty' fish, the flesh resembling lobster meat

—1—

Skin the monkfish, then cut the flesh away from the bone. Put the fillets on a plate, cover and microwave for 6 minutes. Cut the fillets into slices 1 cm (½ in) thick.

—2—

Put the oil, onion, managetout, broccoli, pepper and corn into a large bowl. Mix well then microwave for 4 minutes, stirring after 2 minutes.

—3—

Stir in the fish, sherry and soy sauce. Microwave for 1 minute.

—4—

Mix the cornflour to a smooth paste with one tablespoon water. Stir into the fish/vegetable mixture. When well blended, microwave for 1 minute, then serve.

Braised Lamb Bretonne

Serves 6

1 × 1¼ kg–1½ kg (2½ lb to 3 lb) fillet end leg of lamb
2 cloves garlic, peeled and sliced
2 tablespoons soya oil
1 × 400 g (14 oz) can chopped tomatoes
150 ml (¼ pint) dry cider
a bouquet garni
black pepper to taste
1 × 400 g (14 oz) can flageolet or haricot beans, drained
2 tablespoons chopped parsley

Preparation time:	10 minutes
Cooking time:	40–45 minutes plus standing
Microwave setting:	High

The classic dish of garlic-flavoured lamb with beans and tomatoes, from Brittany

—1—

Trim all the visible fat from the lamb, and make small slits in the skin. Insert a sliver of garlic into each slit.

—2—

Heat the oil in a large heavy frying pan on top of the stove, and quickly brown and seal the meat on all sides. Lift out and drain well.

—3—

Transfer to a large microwave-proof casserole. Add the tomatoes, cider, bouquet garni and pepper.

—4—

Cover and microwave for 35–40 minutes, stirring frequently, and adding the beans for the last 10 minutes of the cooking time. The meat should be tender.

—5—

Leave to stand for 10 minutes, then stir gently and taste for seasoning. Serve the meat thickly sliced, surrounded with the beans sprinkled with parsley.

Baked Bananas in Peach Sauce

Serves 4

4 medium size ripe bananas
1 × 200 g (7 oz) can peaches in natural juice
large pinch ground ginger
1 tablespoon toasted flaked almonds

Preparation time:	5 minutes
Cooking time:	5 minutes
Microwave setting:	High

Peaches canned in natural juice are easily turned into a low-calorie dessert sauce

—1—

Peel the bananas, and slice in half lengthwise. Arrange in a shallow, microwave-proof serving dish.

—2—

Purée the peaches with their juice and the ginger. Pour over the bananas. Cover and microwave for 5 minutes. Serve immediately.

Variation
For those not watching calories, serve with vanilla ice cream.

● To quickly blanch 230 g (8 oz) almonds, cover with 280 ml (½ pint) water. Microwave on high for 2½ to 3 minutes then drain. The skins should slip off easily.
● Don't reheat drinks in plastic cups – they can taint the drink and there is a danger of them melting.

Veal Bolognese with Courgettes, served with tricolour spaghetti (p 34)

Meals in minutes
SUPPERS AND SNACKS

When speed is of the essence, or energy is flagging, the microwave can be your most valuable kitchen gadget. When you arrive home late and tired, it's very tempting to heat up a pre-packed convenience meal. Since too much 'junk' food isn't healthy, it makes sense to make your microwave work hard for you while you relax. And if your family tend to rush in and out at different times, there are many quick meals that can be prepared, left in the fridge, and quickly finished in the microwave. Better than keeping a casserole hot in the oven for hours and hours, wasting fuel and spoiling the food.

Veal Bolognese with Courgettes

Serves 4
1 large onion, finely chopped
2 teaspoons olive oil
1–2 cloves garlic, crushed
450 g (1 lb) lean veal, coarsely minced
350 g (12 oz) tomatoes, quartered and seeded
1 tablespoon tomato purée
1 tablespoon fresh oregano
1 tablespoon flour
50 ml (2 fl oz) white wine
salt and pepper to taste
350 g (12 oz) courgettes,
coarsely grated

Preparation time:	20 minutes
Cooking time:	15–17 minutes
Microwave setting:	High and conventional hob

A low-calorie dish of lean minced veal flavoured with tomatoes and courgettes, served with tricolour spaghetti, available from supermarkets and many delicatessens

—1—

Put the onion and half the oil into a large bowl. Microwave for 2–3 minutes to soften. Stir in the garlic.

—2—

Heat the remaining oil in a non-stick frying pan and quickly brown the veal. Pour off any excess fat, then tip the veal into the onion mixture.

—3—

Stir in the tomatoes, tomato purée, oregano, flour, wine and seasonings. Microwave for 7–8 minutes, stirring the mixture occasionally.

—4—

Put 2 tablespoons of the meat sauce into a non-stick frying pan. Add the grated courgettes and quickly stir-fry over high heat. Stir courgettes into the sauce and taste for seasoning. Serve with boiled spaghetti and grated fresh Parmesan.

Chicken with Grapes and Mild Curry Sauce

Serves 4 to 6
1 × 1½ kg (3–3½ lb) chicken
chicken stock
225 g (8 oz) green seedless grapes, halved
25 g (1 oz) butter or margarine
1½ tablespoons flour
½–1 tablespoon mild curry powder, to taste
salt and pepper to taste
a large pinch saffron or turmeric
150 ml (¼ pint) single cream
To garnish
toasted almonds (optional)
To serve
boiled rice

Preparation time:	15 minutes plus cooling
Cooking time:	35–40 minutes
Microwave setting:	High

Elegant enough for a special supper, this recipe can be prepared ahead and reheated

—1—

Put the chicken into a dish with 5 tablespoons water. Cover with pierced cling film and microwave for 25–30 minutes until the juices run clear (check with your own microwave handbook).

—2—

Keep the juices from the chicken. Leave chicken to cool, then shred the flesh, put in a serving dish and add the grapes.

—3—

Make up the juices from the chicken to 200 ml (7 fl oz) with water. Put the butter, flour, curry powder, seasonings and saffron or turmeric into a jug. Microwave for 1 minute. Stir in stock. Microwave for 6 minutes, whisking every 2 minutes.

—4—

Stir in the cream and taste for seasoning. Pour sauce over the chicken. Microwave for 3 minutes until thoroughly heated. Scatter with toasted almonds and serve with rice.

Emmental Salad

Serves 4
450 g (1 lb) medium-sized leeks
salt
175 g (6 oz) Emmental or Gruyère cheese
175 g (6 oz) cold boiled ham, sliced fairly thickly
6 cooked prunes, stoned
3 tablespoons French dressing

Preparation time:	15 minutes plus draining
Cooking time:	10–20 minutes
Microwave setting:	High

A tasty salad that can be served cold with poppy seed rolls and butter, or hot (without the dressing), making a good accompaniment for omelettes

—1—

Remove the coarse outer green leaves from the leeks (they can be used up in soups). Cut the leeks into three-quarter-inch lengths.

—2—

Put into a bowl with 2 tablespoons water and a little salt and microwave for 10–12 minutes until barely tender. Drain then rinse with cold water. Leave to drain thoroughly.

—3—

Shred the cheese into strips. Cut the ham into strips 2.5 cm (1 in) long. Cut the prunes also into strips.

—4—

Mix the cheese, ham and prunes and leeks together, pour over the dressing and toss well. Serve immediately.

Variation
To serve hot. Put the salad ingredients (without the dressing) into a greased microwave dish. Microwave on medium power for 10 minutes – delicious.

Devon Trout

Serves 4
4 cleaned trout, each about 225 g (8 oz)
salt and pepper to taste
juice of 1 lemon
8 tablespoons double cream
1 tablespoon chopped parsley
1 tablespoon snipped chives
25 g (1 oz) fresh wholemeal breadcrumbs
a well-buttered microwave-proof dish

Preparation time:	5 minutes
Cooking time:	9 minutes plus standing
Microwave setting:	High

An affordable supper treat that's extremely quick to make with the simplest and most delicious ingredients

—1—

Season the trout and lay it in the dish. Add two tablespoons water, lemon juice and cream. Microwave for 4 minutes.

—2—

Carefully turn the fish over and scatter with the herbs and breadcrumbs. Microwave for 4–5 minutes until the fish is almost cooked through.

—3—

Leave to stand, covered, for 3 minutes to finish cooking, then serve with new potatoes and salad, or sauté potatoes and whole green beans.

Cheats' 'Barbecued' Spare Ribs

—2—

Cut the courgettes diagonally into half-inch slices. Mix with tomato pulp and spoon into a microwave-proof serving dish. Microwave for 3–4 minutes until the courgettes are just tender and the sauce thoroughly heated. Sprinkle with parsley and serve immediately.

Variation
Marrow can also be used instead of courgettes. Peel and cut into 2.5 cm (1 in) cubes. Cook as above, but reducing the microwave time. Cauliflower can be cooked in exactly the same way.

Cheats' 'Barbecued' Spare Ribs

Serves 4 to 6
1½ kg (3 lb) pork spare ribs, cut up
For the marinade
3 tablespoons soy sauce
2 tablespoons Branston Spicy Sauce
1 tablespoon Worcestershire sauce
1 tablespoon tomato ketchup
1 tablespoon coarse cut marmalade

Preparation time:	5 minutes plus marinating
Cooking time:	21 minutes
Microwave setting:	High

If you have the time, allow the ribs to marinate for several hours or, better still, overnight

—1—

Put all the marinade ingredients into a bowl and microwave for 1 minute. Stir well and leave to go cold. Add the ribs to the marinade and mix well. Cover and refrigerate for several hours if possible, turning the ribs occasionally.

—2—

Cover the bowl with cling film and microwave for 10 minutes. Baste well and turn the ribs over. Microwave for 10 minutes or until the ribs are tender.

Piquant Courgettes

Serves 6 to 8
450 g (1 lb) ripe tomatoes, skinned
1 medium onion, finely chopped
½ level teaspoon salt
½ level teaspoon paprika
black pepper
a clove of garlic, crushed (or to taste)
1 tablespoon chopped fresh basil
750 g (1½ lb) courgettes
1 tablespoon chopped parsley

Preparation time:	10 minutes
Cooking time:	8–10 minutes
Microwave setting:	High

An ideal accompaniment to both meat and fish dishes, it can also be served as a starter

—1—

Roughly chop the tomatoes and put into a bowl with the onion, seasonings and basil. Microwave for 5–6 minutes, stirring halfway through the cooking time. Purée in a blender or into a food processor.

Apple and Ginger Layer

Serves 6
450 g (1 lb) cooking apples
2 tablespoons ginger syrup
For the sponge
100 g (4 oz) butter or margarine
100 g (4 oz) caster sugar
2 eggs, beaten
50 g (2 oz) self-raising flour, sieved
50 g (2 oz) wholemeal self-raising flour
2–3 teaspoons ground ginger
25 g (1 oz) stem ginger, roughly chopped
3 tablespoons milk
2 tablespoons water
1 × 1.2 litre (2 pint) pudding basin, greased

Preparation time:	20 minutes
Cooking time:	9–10 minutes
Microwave setting:	High

A wintry family favourite to serve with Tangy Lemon Sauce

—1—

Peel, core and slice apples, turn into a bowl and stir in the ginger syrup. Microwave for 2 minutes. Stir and microwave for a further minute.

—2—

To make the sponge, cream butter and sugar until light and fluffy. Gradually beat in the eggs. Fold in the flours and the ground and stem ginger. Stir in the milk and water.

—3—

Place half the apple in a layer in the bottom of the basin. Spoon half the sponge mixture on top and repeat, finishing with a layer of sponge. Cover loosely with cling film and microwave for 3 minutes. Uncover and microwave for a further 3–4 minutes. Turn out and serve with custard.

Tangy Lemon Sauce

Serves 6
grated rind and juice of 1 lemon
a large pinch of cornflour
50 g (2 oz) caster sugar
2 egg yolks

Preparation time:	5 minutes
Cooking time:	6 minutes
Microwave setting:	High

This slightly sharp sauce subtly counteracts the sweetness of the pudding

—1—

Put the lemon juice into a measuring jug and make up to 150 ml (¼ pint) with water. Stir in the cornflour and lemon rind and microwave for 2 minutes.

—2—

Stir well, then mix in the sugar and egg yolks. Microwave for 4 minutes or until the sauce thickens. Serve hot.

● While testing and developing the hundreds of recipes in this book we've discovered many short cuts, useful facts and new ideas. We're happy to pass them all on.
● Always underestimate the cooking times until you get to know your microwave. It's very easy to overcook or spoil food. You can always return the food to the microwave and cook for a further few minutes if this proves necessary.
● To dry homegrown herbs for use during the winter, microwave them on high for 25 seconds.
● To soften ice cream or butter straight from the freezer, microwave on defrost for 30 seconds to 1 minute.
● Reheat toast by microwaving on high for 20 to 25 seconds per slice. If you have a non-metallic toast rack, pop the toast into the microwave while still in the rack.
● As there is no control over the fat temperature, you cannot deep-fry in the microwave. However, you can cook 'oven chips'. Line a plate with a double layer of kitchen paper. Take 225 g (8 oz) of oven chips from the freezer and spread evenly in a single layer. Cook for 6 minutes on full power, and do not cover.

Rhubarb and Ginger Dreams

Serves 6
450 g (1 lb) fresh trimmed rhubarb
50 g (2 oz) demerara sugar
2 level tablespoons custard powder
1 level tablespoon caster sugar
300 ml (½ pint) milk
50 g (2 oz) ginger nuts
150 ml (¼ pint) whipping cream
1 tablespoon brandy
6 glasses

Preparation time:	25 minutes plus cooling
Cooking time:	16½–21½ minutes
Microwave setting:	High and Medium

A creamy purée of fruit layered with ginger biscuit crumbs and flavoured with a hint of brandy

—1—

Wipe the rhubarb and cut into 2.5 cm (1 in) lengths. Put into a bowl with 2 tablespoons water. Cover with pierced cling film and microwave on high power for 10–15 minutes until pulpy.

—2—

Add the demerara sugar and cook on medium power for 2½ minutes. Cool slightly then purée in a blender or processor. Leave to go cold.

—3—

To make the custard, mix the custard powder to a paste with the caster sugar and 3 tablespoons of the milk. Microwave the remaining milk on high power for 2 minutes, and stir into the paste. Microwave on high power for 2 minutes, whisking every 30 seconds. Leave to cool.

—4—

Put the ginger nuts into a polythene bag and crush with a rolling pin.

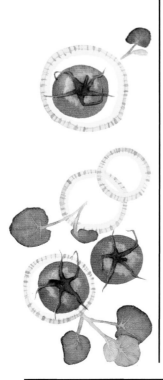

—5—

Whip the cream until it holds its shape then fold into the cold rhubarb with the cold custard. Layer in the glasses with the ginger nut crumbs. Sprinkle each layer of crumbs with a drop of brandy. Top with a scattering of ginger nut crumbs.

Tasty Layer

Serves 4 to 6
1 tablespoon soya oil
450 g (1 lb) lean minced beef
1 large onion, finely chopped
1 × 400 g (14 oz) can tomatoes
1 teaspoon dried mixed herbs
salt and pepper to taste
1 kg (2 lb) potatoes, peeled
450 g (1 lb) carrots, peeled and sliced
25 g (1 oz) butter

Preparation time:	20 minutes
Cooking time:	21–28 minutes
Microwave setting:	High

—1—

Heat the oil in a frying pan. Add minced beef and onion and cook on a high heat until browned. Stir in tomatoes, roughly chopped, and heat through. Stir in seasoning.

—2—

Slice potatoes ¼ inch thick and put in a large microwave-proof bowl. Add 5 tablespoons boiling water, cover and microwave for 3–5 minutes, until just tender. Strain. Place the carrots in a bowl, add 2 tablespoons boiling water and microwave for 5–7 minutes. Drain.

—3—

In a microwave-proof dish layer up the savoury mince, carrots and potatoes, finishing with a layer of potatoes.

—4—

Microwave the butter for 1–1½ minutes until melted. Brush over the potatoes. Microwave for 12–15 minutes.

Lamb with Peach and Hazelnut Stuffing

Serves 4 to 6
2 boned breasts of lamb, each weighing about
450 g (1 lb)
For the stuffing
2 tablespoons soya oil
230 g (8 oz) dried peaches, roughly chopped
110 g (4 oz) toasted hazelnuts, chopped
85 g (3 oz) fresh wholemeal
breadcrumbs
110 g (4 oz) California
seedless raisins
salt, pepper and cumin to taste
1½ eggs, size 3, beaten
2 tablespoons milk

Preparation time: 10 minutes
Cooking time: about 25 minutes
Microwave setting: High

Boned breast of lamb is available from large supermarkets or your local butcher.

—*1*—

Put the oil into a medium-sized mixing bowl. Microwave on 'high' for 40 seconds. Stir in the peaches, nuts, breadcrumbs and raisins. Stir in the seasonings, eggs and milk to make a moist stuffing. Lay the boned lamb breasts flat on a board and divide the mixture between them. Spread the stuffing evenly over the meat, then roll up each breasts, fairly tightly, and tie securely with string. Rub a little cumin over each piece of lamb.

—*2*—

Put the lamb on a special meat rack set over a tray (or in a shallow dish). Microwave on 'high' for 5 minutes. Baste the meat well, then microwave on 'high' for a further 8 minutes or until the meat is almost cooked. Wrap the meat in foil and leave to stand for 10 minutes.

—*3*—

Serve thickly sliced with gravy or redcurrant jelly and a green vegetable.

Gammon and Leek Suet Roll

Serves 4
For the filling
40 g (1½ oz) butter
2 medium leeks, thinly sliced
1 medium onion, thinly sliced
40 g (1½ oz) plain flour
300 ml (½ pint) chicken or vegetable stock
225 g (8 oz) gammon steak
salt, pepper and nutmeg to taste
For the pastry
225 g (8 oz) self-raising flour
1 teaspoon salt
2 teaspoons mustard powder
75 g (3 oz) shredded suet

Preparation time: 25 minutes
Cooking time: 16–20 minutes plus standing
Microwave setting: High

—*1*—

Put the butter into a jug with the leeks and onion. Microwave for 3–4 minutes or until the vegetables are soft.

—*2*—

Stir in the flour followed by the stock. Cover and microwave for 6 minutes, stirring every 2 minutes. Shred the gammon and stir into the sauce with seasoning to taste.

—*3*—

Sift the flour, salt and mustard powder into a mixing bowl. Stir in the suet. Add just enough cold water to make a soft, pliable dough. Turn on to a lightly floured work surface and knead lightly until the dough comes together.

—*4*—

Roll out to an oblong roughly 30 by 23 cm (12 by 9 in). Spread with the filling and roll up loosely. Wrap loosely in cling film then put into a shallow baking dish. Microwave for 7–10 minutes. Leave to stand for 2 minutes, unwrap and serve.

Moules à la Marinière

Serves 2
450 g (1 lb) fresh mussels
1 small onion, very finely chopped
2 tablespoons dry white wine
2 tablespoons water
2 small bay leaves
salt and freshly ground black pepper
1 level tablespoon chopped parsley
2 microwave-proof deep soup plates
To accompany
French bread

Preparation time:	10 minutes
Cooking time:	3 minutes
Microwave setting:	High

A favourite from France

Scrub the mussels really well under cold running water, discarding any which are not tightly shut or any that float.

—*2*—

Put half into each plate, sprinkle half the chopped onion over each, then add half the white wine and water and a small bay leaf to each. Cover with pierced cling film.

—*3*—

Microwave one at a time. Microwave for 1½ minutes, turn the dish and microwave for a further 1½ minutes. Season to taste, garnish with chopped parsley. (All the mussels should open; discard any which remain closed.)

● It's easy to make your own chicken or meat stock in the microwave. Put 455 g (1 lb) chicken or meat bones in a large bowl with a chopped onion and carrot plus a bouquet garni. Add 1.15 litre (2 pint) boiling water to cover, then cover bowl with pierced cling film and microwave on high for 15 minutes.
Stir the stock, then cover again and microwave on defrost for 20 to 30 minutes. Leave to cool before straining and degreasing. Use the stock for soups, gravies, sauces and stews. Cooled stock can be skimmed and frozen.

Special Steak and Kidney Pudding

Serves 4 to 6
For the filling
450 g (1 lb) lean frying steak, cubed
225 g (8 oz) lamb's kidneys, cored and cubed
2 tablespoons seasoned flour
2 tablespoons soya oil
1 medium onion, finely chopped
25 g (1 oz) butter or margarine
150 ml (¼ pint) stock and red wine mixed
50 g (2 oz) walnut pieces
grated rind of ½ orange
salt and pepper to taste
For the suet crust
350 g (12 oz) self raising flour
1 level teaspoon baking powder
½ teaspoon each salt and freshly ground black pepper
175 g (6 oz) chopped suet
2 tablespoons chopped fresh herbs (parsley, chives, thyme, marjoram)
1 × 1.75 litre (3 pint) pudding basin

Preparation time:	30 minutes, plus cooling
Cooking time:	30–35 minutes
Microwave setting:	High

For extra flavour, we've added chopped fresh herbs to the suet crust, and red wine and walnuts to the meat filling. Cooking suet puddings is both quick and simple in the microwave

—*1*—

Toss the steak and kidney in the seasoned flour. Heat the oil in a non-stick frying pan and quickly brown the meat.

Put the onion and butter in a bowl. Cover with cling film and microwave for 3 minutes. Add the meat with any excess seasoned flour and the remaining filling ingredients. Cover and microwave for 10–12 minutes, until the meat is tender. Stir, then leave to cool.

—3—

To make the suet crust, mix all the ingredients together in a large bowl. Stir in a scant 300 ml (½ pint) cold water to make a firm dough. Roll two-thirds of the dough to a circle and use to line the basin, easing into the base. Roll out the remaining dough to a circle the size of the top of the basin to form the lid.

—4—

Fill the suet crust-lined basin with the meat filling. Dampen the rim of the suet crust with water and cover with the lid, pressing to seal firmly. Cover loosely with cling film and microwave for 12–15 minutes. Turn out and serve immediately with extra gravy.

Orange-Glazed Pork Chops

Serves 6
6 pork loin chops
2 oranges
3 tablespoons demerara sugar
1 tablespoon mustard powder
salt and pepper to taste
orange wedges and watercress to garnish

Preparation time: 15 minutes
Cooking time: 9–10 minutes
Microwave setting: High

Strips of citrus rind can be quickly made using a special 'canelle' knife, available from kitchen shops. It has five holes along the top edge and a short handle, and pares rind thinly

—1—

Trim the chops to remove the excess fat. Grate the rind from one orange and mix well with the sugar and mustard powder. Use a canelle knife to remove strips of orange rind from the second orange (or peel off the rind using a vegetable peeler and thinly slice the rind into needle-like shreds). Stir the rind into the sugar mixture with the juice from both oranges.

—2—

Put the chops into a dish and microwave for 7 minutes.

—3—

Pour over the orange sauce. Cover and microwave for 2–3 minutes until the meat is cooked and the sauce is boiling. Garnish and serve with jacket potatoes or rice.

Orange-Glazed Pork Chops

Potted Fish Ramekins

Serves 4
225 g (8 oz) fresh salmon steaks
1 × 450 g (1 lb) trout, cleaned
50 ml (2 fl oz) dry white wine
a slice of lemon
a bouquet garni
6 peppercorns
100 g (4 oz) unsalted butter
salt, pepper, cayenne, lemon juice to taste
To garnish
cucumber slices
4 ramekin dishes

Preparation time:	20 minutes plus chilling
Cooking time:	7–9 minutes plus standing
Microwave setting:	High

For a lazy supper around the fire or television, this tasty fish paté served with toast and salad is an ideal treat

—1—

Put the salmon and trout into a microwave-proof baking dish together with the wine, lemon slice, bouquet garni and peppercorns, plus 50 ml (2 fl oz) cold water.

—2—

Cover with cling film and microwave for 6–8 minutes. Leave to stand for 3 minutes, then unwrap and leave to cool. Remove the skin and bones from the fish. Flake the flesh into a bowl and pound or process with half of the butter. Season to taste with salt, pepper, cayenne and plenty of lemon juice. Spoon the mixture into four ramekins and press down well.

—3—

Put the remaining butter into a small bowl or jug and microwave for 1 minute. Strain through a paper coffee filter or a small sieve lined with kitchen paper. Pour the clarified butter over the potted fish and chill. Garnish with cucumber slices.

Pasta Butterflies with Tuna

Serves 4
225 g (8 oz) pasta shapes or spaghetti or macaroni
1 × 300 g (10.6 oz) can condensed mushroom soup
150 ml (¼ pint) single cream
1 × 200 g (7 oz) tin tuna or salmon trout, drained
2 tablespoons chopped parsley
black pepper to taste

Preparation time:	5 minutes
Cooking time:	12 minutes
Microwave setting:	High

Dried pasta comes in all sorts of shapes and sizes – we used *farfallini*, or butterflies, but *rotini* (spirals), *conchiglie* (shells) or *ruote* (wheels) are equally good in creamy mushroom and tuna or salmon trout sauce

—1—

Put the pasta into a large bowl of boiling water and leave to stand for 1 minute, then microwave for 10 minutes until just tender (al dente).

—2—

Drain well and put into a large serving bowl. Add the remaining ingredients and toss gently. Microwave for 2 minutes until piping hot. Toss again and serve immediately.

Chilli Stuffing for Tacos

Serves 4
1 tablespoon soya or olive oil
1 clove garlic, crushed
1 large onion, finely chopped
1–2 tablespoons chilli powder
½ teaspoon ground cumin
½ teaspoon oregano
½ teaspoon cinnamon
salt, pepper and cayenne to taste
450 g (1 lb) lean minced beef
1 × 400 g (14 oz) can red kidney beans
1 × 400 g (14 oz) can tomatoes
1 green pepper, cored and finely chopped
4 tablespoons tomato purée

Preparation time:	15 minutes
Cooking time:	34–37 minutes plus standing
Microwave setting:	High

Use this spicy filling to stuff ready-made taco shells, available from large supermarkets or delicatessens – allow about two shells per person. Top with sour cream, lettuce and grated cheese. The same mixture can be used to fill ready-cooked pancakes or baked jacket potatoes

—1—

In a large bowl, mix together the oil, garlic, onion, chilli powder, cumin, oregano, cinnamon and a little seasoning. Microwave for 4–5 minutes. Stir in 2 tablespoons water. Microwave for 2 minutes, then leave to stand for 3 minutes.

—2—

Stir in the minced beef, until thoroughly mixed and there are no lumps. Spoon into a shallow baking dish. Microwave for 8–10 minutes, stirring after 4 minutes to break up the meat. Stir in the remaining ingredients. Cover with cling film and microwave for 20 minutes, stirring twice to thoroughly blend. Taste for seasoning.

—3—

Spoon the Chilli mixture into the taco shells and serve each with a spoonful of soured cream, a little shredded lettuce and some grated cheese.

● When heating two meals together, separate them with a plate-stacking ring and cover the top plate with cling film*, or an upturned plate or plate cover.
● Do not cover pastry items as they will be soggy.

Sausage Stuffed Mushrooms

Serves 4 to 6
8 large mushrooms
25 g (1 oz) butter or margarine
1 small onion, finely chopped
225 g (8 oz) Cumberland sausage or other well-flavoured sausages, skinned
100 g (4 oz) fresh wholemeal breadcrumbs
1 tablespoon chopped fresh parsley
1 clove garlic, crushed
salt and pepper to taste
1 egg, beaten

Preparation time:	10 minutes
Cooking time:	8–12 minutes
Microwave setting:	High

Large flat mushrooms are excellent stuffed with a savoury sausagemeat filling and served with hot scrambled eggs and bacon

—1—

Wipe the mushrooms, remove the stalks and chop them roughly. Put the chopped stalks into a bowl with the butter and onion. Cover and microwave for 3–4 minutes.

—2—

Stir in the sausagemeat, breadcrumbs, parsley, garlic, seasoning and herbs. When thoroughly mixed, divide the stuffing between the eight mushrooms.

—3—

Evenly arrange the mushrooms in a circle on a buttered, microwave-proof plate. Microwave for 5–8 minutes or until the mushrooms are tender and the filling is completely cooked. Serve immediately.

Pasta Marco

Serves 4 to 6

225 g (8 oz) pasta spirals
a large pinch of salt
1 tablespoon olive or vegetable oil
450 g (1 lb) tomatoes, skinned and chopped
1 large green pepper, cored and chopped
1 large yellow pepper, cored and chopped
175 g (6 oz) garlic sausage, diced (optional)
175 g (6 oz) mature Cheddar cheese, diced
salt and pepper to taste
1 tablespoon chopped fresh herbs

Preparation time: 10 minutes
Cooking time: 13–15 minutes
Microwave setting: High

Prepare the vegetables while the pasta is cooking and you'll have a very quick and easy meal

—1—

Put the pasta into a large non-metallic bowl with the salt, oil and 900 ml (1½ pints) boiling water. Microwave for 10–12 minutes.

—2—

Strain the pasta, then rinse with boiling water. Stir in the remaining ingredients except herbs. Microwave for 3 minutes to heat through and melt the cheese. Toss gently with the chopped fresh herbs before serving.

Trout en Papillote;
Pasta Marco; Spiced
Pear Ring

Trout en Papillote

Serves 2

2 cleaned rainbow trout, each about 200 g (7 oz)
15 g (½ oz) butter or margarine
1 small grapefruit
25 g (1 oz) browned hazelnuts, roughly chopped
25 g (1 oz) mushrooms, wiped and chopped
2 teaspoons chopped parsley
salt and pepper to taste

Preparation time: 20 minutes
Cooking time: 8½–10½ minutes
Microwave setting: Medium, then High

Fish wrapped in greaseproof paper is speedily and cleanly cooked by microwave

— *1* —

Wipe the trout, and trim off the tail and fins using scissors.

— *2* —

Place the butter in a bowl and microwave on medium power for 30 seconds to melt it. Grate the rind from the grapefruit and stir into the butter. Remove the pith from the grapefruit, and divide the flesh into segments. Chop this and stir into the butter with the nuts, mushrooms and parsley. Add seasoning to taste. Spoon the stuffing into the body cavity of each trout.

— *3* —

Cut two pieces of greaseproof paper, each roughly 30 × 23 cm (12 × 9 in) Grease the paper lightly. Then use to wrap each fish loosely, folding the edges of the paper together on top, and twisting the ends.

— *4* —

Place the fish on a plate and microwave on high power for 8–10 minutes, depending on size. The flesh will flake easily once the fish has cooked through.

Spiced Pear Ring

Serves 6

75 g (3 oz) butter or margarine, softened
2 tablespoons black treacle
2 tablespoons golden syrup
2 teaspoons ground ginger
1 teaspoon mixed spice
175 g (6 oz) plain flour
50 g (2 oz) caster sugar
1 teaspoon bicarbonate of soda
a pinch of salt
1 egg, beaten
1 × 400 g (14 oz) can pear halves in syrup
1 × 1.2–1.75 litre (2–3 pint) microwave-ware or Pyrex cooking ring mould, about 24 cm (9½ in) diameter

Preparation time: 15 minutes
Cooking time: 11–12 minutes plus standing
Microwave setting: High

A cooking ring ensures the even cooking of this unusual sponge pudding

— *1* —

Place the butter or margarine, treacle, syrup, ginger and mixed spice in a jug. Microwave for 1–2 minutes.

— *2* —

Sieve the remaining dry ingredients into a large bowl. Stir in the melted mixture, the egg and 6 tablespoons of syrup from the can of fruit.

— *3* —

Beat well for 3 minutes. Slice the drained pears and arrange around the base of the ring mould.

— *4* —

Spoon over the sponge mixture. Microwave for 10 minutes, then leave to stand for 5 minutes. Turn out and serve immediately.

Hot Tuna Stuffed Pittas

Serves 4
4 wholewheat pitta breads
For the stuffing
1 × 185 g (6½ oz) can tuna in oil
175 g (6 oz) long grain rice, cooked
6 spring onions, trimmed
1 large tomato
6 tablespoons mayonnaise
salt and pepper to taste

Preparation time: 10 minutes
Cooking time: 2 minutes
Microwave setting: High

The rice and tuna stuffing is also good cold served as a salad

—1—

Cut each pitta bread in half, then split open to form pockets.

—2—

Drain the tuna and reserve the oil. Flake the fish and put into a bowl with the rice. Finely slice the spring onions and chop the tomato. Add to rice, mix well.

—3—

Stir the reserved tuna oil into the mayonnaise and mix this into the stuffing with plenty of seasoning. (This stuffing can be prepared overnight, covered and stored in the fridge). Spoon the stuffing into the pittas and put on to a plate. Microwave for 2 minutes until heated right through.

Chicken with Almonds

Serves 6
2 tablespoons soya oil
25 g (1 oz) unsalted butter
2 large onions, thinly sliced
50 g (2 oz) flaked almonds
40 g (1½ oz) flour
300 ml (½ pint) boiling chicken stock
6 chicken portions, skinned
salt and pepper to taste
To garnish
25 g (1 oz) toasted flaked almonds

Preparation time: 5 minutes
Cooking time: 25–32 minutes
Microwave setting: High

As it takes so little preparation, this is an ideal dish to serve for a mid-week occasion

—1—

Put the oil, butter and onions into a bowl. Microwave for 6 minutes until tender. Add the flaked almonds and flour and stir well. Stir in the chicken stock. Microwave for 4–6 minutes, stirring halfway through, to make a thickened sauce. Add a little seasoning if it is required.

—2—

Put the chicken joints into a dish and pour over the sauce. Microwave for 15–20 minutes, turning the joints a couple of times during the cooking. The exact cooking time will depend on the size and type of chicken joint.

—3—

Scatter with toasted flaked almonds before serving with broccoli and rice or noodles.

● Small amounts of vegetables (up to 455 g/1 lb) can be successfully blanched in the microwave ready for freezing. To do this, put the vegetables into a large bowl with 85 ml (3 fl oz) water. Cover with cling film and microwave on high for 4 to 6 minutes, stirring occasionally. Drain the vegetables then plunge immediately into iced water to stop the cooking process. Drain well, then open freeze on trays before bagging, dating and labelling.

● When baking food such as whole jacket potatoes or apples, pierce the skin several times with a cocktail stick or skewer to prevent them bursting in the microwave.

● To toast desiccated coconut, spread 110 g (4 oz) evenly on a large plate. Microwave on high for 5 minutes, stirring frequently.

● For the best results, you should reheat any fibrous vegetables – asparagus, broccoli and so on – in a sauce. Don't reheat fried foods as they become soggy.

Turkey Divan

Serves 6

750 g (1½ lb) cooked turkey or chicken meat, cubed
450 g (1 lb) fresh broccoli, trimmed
1 × 300 g (10.4 oz) can condensed cream of chicken soup
200 ml (7 fl oz) single cream or top of the milk
150 ml (¼ pint) mayonnaise
2 oz Gruyère cheese, grated
2 tablespoons lemon juice
1 tablespoon curry paste or to taste
1 tablespoon cashew nuts, toasted
1 tablespoon Parmesan cheese, grated
15 g (½ oz) butter

Preparation time:	15 minutes
Cooking time:	17–20 minutes
Microwave setting:	High

Initially this seems a strange combination of ingredients, but it's delicious and is a very popular recipe in America

—1—

Put the broccoli florets in a dish, stalks upwards. Cover with cling film and microwave for 3 minutes.

—2—

Mix the soup with the cream, mayonnaise, Gruyère cheese, lemon juice and curry paste.

—3—

Arrange the broccoli in the base of a gratin dish. Cover with the turkey cubes, then sprinkle with the nuts. Spoon over the sauce to cover.

—4—

Sprinkle with the Parmesan and dot with butter. Microwave for 12–15 minutes until piping hot. Quickly brown under a hot grill before serving.

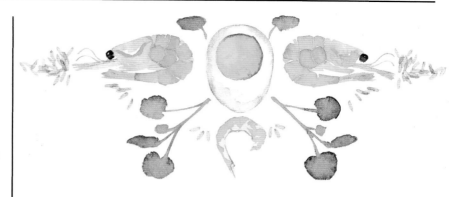

Piperade

Serves 3 to 4

1 small onion, finely sliced
2 green peppers, cored and thinly sliced
225 g (8 oz) tomatoes, peeled and chopped
½ teaspoon dried basil
salt and pepper to taste
3 eggs, beaten

Preparation time:	10 minutes
Cooking time:	9–10 minutes plus standing
Microwave setting:	High

A marvellous combination of tomatoes, softened peppers and fluffy scrambled eggs, this is a speciality imported from the Basque country

—1—

Put the onion and pepper into a mixing bowl. Microwave for 5–6 minutes, stirring twice during the cooking time, until soft.

—2—

Add the tomatoes. Microwave for 2 minutes.

—3—

Drain off any excess liquid and stir in the basil, seasoning and the beaten eggs. Microwave for about 2 minutes or until the eggs are softly scrambled. You will need to stir the mixture every 20 to 30 seconds.

—4—

Leave to stand for 1 minute then serve in individual dishes with fresh, crusty bread.

Top:
*Tagliatelle
with Chicken Liver
Sauce*
Bottom:
*Tagliatelle with
Chicken Asparagus
Sauce*

Chicken Asparagus Sauce

Serves 4

230 g (8 oz) meat from a cooked barbecued
chicken
4 shallots, chopped
15 g (½ oz) butter or margarine
1 stick celery, chopped
280 g (10 oz) can condensed asparagus soup
140 ml (¼ pint) single cream
pepper to taste
40 g (1½ oz) Cheddar cheese, grated

Preparation time:	10 minutes
Cooking time:	about 15 minutes
Microwave setting:	High

For a special occasion garnish with canned
asparagus spears, chopped

—1—

Chop the chicken, discarding any skin. Put
the shallots, butter and celery in a bowl and
microwave for 4–5 minutes, stirring after 2
minutes, until softened. Stir in the soup
and the cream and season with pepper
only.

—2—

Cover and microwave for 2 minutes, stirring after 1 minute. Add the chicken and
microwave for 2 minutes (again stirring
after 1 minute). Stir in the cheese, then
leave to stand, covered, for 5 minutes.

—3—

Pour the sauce over hot pasta, then toss
lightly to mix.

Anchovy and Three-Bean Sauce

Serves 4

15 g (½ oz) butter or margarine or a tablespoon
olive oil
1 large onion, chopped
1 clove garlic, crushed
40 g (1½ oz) can anchovy fillets, drained and
chopped
440 g (15½ oz) can three-bean mix, drained and
rinsed
2 tomatoes, skinned and chopped
pepper to taste
6 fresh spinach leaves, washed and shredded
(optional)

Preparation time:	15 minutes
Cooking time:	about 7 minutes
Microwave setting:	High

Cans of pre-cooked beans are a useful addition to a store cupboard, as they can easily
be turned into a tasty meal

—1—

Place the butter, margarine or oil, onion,
garlic and anchovies in a bowl. Cover and
microwave for 3–4 minutes, stirring after 1
minute, until the onion is soft.

48

—2—

Add the beans and tomatoes. Mix well, then cover and microwave for 2–3 minutes until the mixture is thoroughly heated. Taste for seasoning. Stir through the shredded spinach and spoon over the cooked pasta.

Melbury Sauce

Serves 4
1 tablespoon olive oil or vegetable oil
1 small onion, thinly sliced
1 clove garlic, crushed
680 g (1½ lb) tomatoes, skinned and chopped (or 2 x 395 g (14 oz) cans plum tomatoes, drained and chopped)
2 tablespoons chopped fresh basil or parsley
2 tablespoons dry white wine (omit if using canned tomatoes)
salt and pepper to taste
60 g (2 oz) stoned black olives, chopped
140 g (5 oz) packet Melbury cheese (rind removed), cubed

Preparation time: 20 minutes
Cooking time: 14–15 minutes
Microwave setting: High

The creamy taste of Melbury cheese works well in this rich sauce. For extra piquancy the Melbury can be replaced with an equal quantity of ripe Camembert

—1—

Put the oil, onion and garlic in a bowl and microwave for 2 minutes (stirring after 1 minute) until the onion is soft.

—2—

Stir in the tomatoes, herbs, wine (if using) and seasoning. Cover and microwave for 6–7 minutes, stirring halfway through the cooking time, until the sauce is thick and pulpy. Stir in the olives and cheese. Cover and leave to stand for 5 minutes to melt the cheese.

—3—

Add to cooked pasta and toss gently. (The sauce is excellent served with shell pasta.)

Chicken Liver Sauce

Serves 4
230 g (8 oz) chicken livers
1 tablespoon seasoned flour
1 clove garlic, crushed (optional)
3 tablespoons soya oil
1 stick celery, chopped
1 carrot, chopped
1 green pepper, cored and chopped
a 425 g (15 oz) can plum tomatoes
1 teaspoon dried oregano
1 teaspoon dried basil
salt and pepper to taste
2 tablespoons grated Parmesan cheese

For a milder, more creamy flavour, soak the chicken livers in milk for 20 minutes before draining and using in this tasty and nutritious sauce

—1—

Pat the chicken livers dry, then trim if necessary. Toss in seasoned flour. Put into a bowl with the garlic and one tablespoon of the oil. Cover and microwave on 'high' for 2 to 3 minutes, stirring after 1 minute. Remove from the bowl.

—2—

Add the vegetables with the remaining oil to the bowl. Cover and microwave on 'high' for 6 to 8 minutes, until the vegetables are tender. Add the chopped tomatoes and their juice with a tablespoon water (or vegetable stock), the herbs and the liver.

—3—

Cover and microwave on 'high' for 5 to 6 minutes, stirring halfway through, until the liver is cooked but tender. (Over-cooking will toughen the liver.) Taste for seasoning.

—4—

Pour the sauce over the pasta, then sprinkle with Parmesan before serving.

Tagliatelle Carbonara

Serves 4
230 g (8 oz) tagliatelle
salt and pepper to taste
230 g (8 oz) streaky bacon, rind removed
2 egg yolks
5 tablespoons finely grated fresh Parmesan
cheese
85 ml (3 fl oz) double cream
black pepper to taste
To garnish
fresh parsley

Preparation time: 5 minutes
Cooking time: about 20 minutes
Microwave setting: High

A favourite Italian classic using dried tagliatelle or egg noodles. Reduce the cooking time when using fresh pasta

—1—

Put the pasta into a large bowl of boiling water. Microwave for 10–12 minutes or until just tender, 'al dente', stirring gently after 5 minutes. Drain and rinse thoroughly with hot water, drain again, and put into a warmed serving bowl.

—2—

Put the bacon on a bacon rack or on crumpled kitchen paper and microwave for 1 minute per rasher, until crispy. Snip into small pieces.

—3—

Beat the egg yolks with the Parmesan, cream and pepper. Stir into the pasta with the bacon. Microwave for 2–3 minutes. Stir gently, then serve, garnished with parsley.

Crab Bisque

Serves 6
40 g (1½ oz) unsalted butter or margarine
1 medium onion, chopped
1 clove garlic, crushed
2 large carrots, sliced
1 large leek, sliced
75 g (3 oz) dark crab meat, thawed
salt, pepper and cayenne to taste
75 g (3 oz) white crab meat thawed
To complete
2 tablespoons dry sherry (optional)
a little chopped parsley

Preparation time: 15 minutes
Cooking time: 21–23 minutes
Microwave setting: High

Frozen crab meat can be used to make luxuriously delicious yet filling soup

—1—

Put the butter into a large bowl. Microwave for 1 minute. Stir in the onion and garlic with a pinch of salt and pepper. Microwave for 2 minutes, stirring halfway through, until tender.

—2—

Add the sliced carrots and leek to the bowl with the dark crab meat, 1.2 litres (2 pints) water (or vegetable stock) and a little seasoning. Microwave for 15 minutes or until the vegetables are really tender.

—3—

Liquidize the soup until smooth. Stir in the white crab meat and taste for seasoning. Spoon into individual soup bowls and reheat – about 3–5 minutes. Stir a little sherry into each bowl before serving and sprinkle with the chopped parsley. Serve with french bread.

Arbroath Smokies in Cream

Serves 4
1 kg (2 lb) Arbroath smokies
1 slice each onion and carrot
1 bay leaf
6 peppercorns
50 ml (2 fl oz) dry vermouth
25 g (1 oz) butter
25 g (1 oz) flour
ground nutmeg and pepper to taste
4 tablespoons freshly grated Parmesan cheese
2 tablespoons double cream
1 tablespoon dried breadcrumbs
4 microwave-proof ramekins

Preparation time: 10 minutes
Cooking time: 12 minutes
Microwave setting: High

Arbroath smokies have a very distinctive flavour, but kippers or smoked haddock can also be used for this tasty dish

—1—

Put the fish into a shallow dish with the onion, carrot, bay leaf, peppercorns and 150 ml (¼ pint) water. Cover with cling film and microwave for 6 minutes.

—2—

Drain and reserve the liquid. Discard the flavourings, and the skin and bones from the fish. Flake the flesh. Make up the fish liquid to 300 ml (½ pint) with the vermouth and milk if necessary.

—3—

Put the butter in a jug. Microwave for 1 minute. Stir in the flour, seasonings and the liquid. Microwave for 3 minutes, stirring halfway through. Add the Parmesan, cream and flaked fish. Spoon into four ramekins. Microwave for 2 minutes. Scatter each with breadcrumbs and brown quickly under a hot grill.

Turkey Pilau

Serves 6
450 g (1 lb) cooked turkey meat, weighed without skin and bones, chopped into bite-sized pieces
3 medium onions, thinly sliced
100 g (4 oz) butter or margarine
1 level tablespoon strong curry powder
350 g (12 oz) long grain rice
1 clove garlic, crushed
12 cardamom seeds
1 × 5 cm (2 in) piece of cinnamon stick
6 cloves
8 allspice berries
½ level teaspoon turmeric
600 ml (1 pint) turkey or chicken stock
100 g (4 oz) seedless California raisins
salt and pepper to taste
3 hard-boiled eggs
50 g (2 oz) cashew nuts, toasted

Preparation time: 15 minutes
Cooking time: 23–24 minutes
Microwave setting: High

Turkey portions are ideal for an economical midweek treat. Left-over meat from your Christmas turkey is excellent cooked in a spicy pilau

—1—

Put the onions into a large bowl with the butter and microwave for 6 minutes, until soft. Stir in the curry powder, rice, garlic and spices. Microwave for 2 minutes. Stir in the stock and microwave for 12 minutes.

—2—

Stir gently then mix in the turkey and raisins, and seasoning to taste. Spoon into a serving dish. Microwave for 3–4 minutes, until piping hot.

—3—

Remove whole spices if wished. Chop the eggs and sprinkle over the pilau with the nuts. Serve immediately with chutney and a salad.

● Meals on plates reheat perfectly in the microwave; you can even reheat bacon and eggs. But there are a few rules to follow for a uniform distribution of heat:
● Place thin foods in the centre of the plate and thicker foods towards the outside.
● It's best to reheat only two meals at a time.

Crab Cioppino (p 54)

Holiday treats for all WEEKEND WONDERS

For weekends you would rather spend in the sun, or out with the family, at home or on holiday, a microwave will give you much more freedom to be out enjoying yourself. What's more, you don't have to resort to uninspiring food as a result. Microwave cooking really is helpful on warm days because not only does it cut down on the cooking time, but as a microwave oven doesn't generate heat in the kitchen both it and you stay cool. Here are a variety of dishes to serve as weekend and holiday treats for all the family, including the cook.

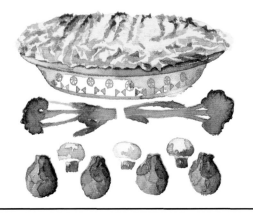

Crab Cioppino

Serves 4 to 6

2 tablespoons olive oil
1 medium onion, finely chopped
1 red pepper, cored and finely chopped
2 cloves garlic, crushed
50 g (2 oz) mushrooms, diced
1 × 400 g (14 oz) can tomatoes, chopped
2 tablespoons red wine (optional)
1½ tablespoons tomato purée
salt, pepper, tabasco and
caster sugar, all to taste
a bouquet garni
6 jumbo prawns, peeled
1 × 450 g (1 lb) cooked crab, cleaned
225 g (8 oz) clams, cleaned and scrubbed
2 large scallops
100 g (4 oz) fillet haddock, sea bass or bream
100 g (4 oz) monkfish tail fillet
2 tablespoons chopped fresh herbs

Preparation time:	40 minutes
Cooking time:	23½–25½ minutes
Microwave setting:	High

Fisherman's Wharf in San Francisco is the place to eat crab and other seafood delicacies in America. This wonderful fish stew is their most popular dish

—1—

Put the oil, onion and pepper in a large bowl and microwave for 6 minutes, stirring every 2 minutes. Add the garlic and mushrooms. Stir well, then microwave for 1 minute.

—2—

Stir in the tomatoes with their juice, the wine, tomato purée, seasonings and bouquet garni. Microwave for 6 minutes. Remove the bouquet garni, then purée the sauce in a blender or processor and return it to the bowl.

—3—

Cut each prawn in two or three pieces. Crack the crab claws using fish- or nutcrackers or a meat mallet, and break into large pieces. Add the crab claws (unshelled) with the rest of the crabmeat and the clams to the sauce. Cover and microwave for 2½

minutes or until the clams have all opened (discard any that remain closed after a little more cooking).

—4—

Halve the scallops, and cut the fish fillets into large chunks or cubes. Stir into the sauce with the prawns. Microwave for 8–10 minutes, stirring every 2 minutes, until all the fish is cooked.

—5—

Taste for seasoning, then stir in the herbs. Serve with plenty of warm crusty bread or garlic bread.

Hearty Cottage Pie

Serves 4 to 6

1 tablespoon soya oil
1 large onion, finely chopped
1 large carrot, finely diced
450 g (1 lb) lean minced beef
2 tablespoons chopped parsley
2 tablespoons Worcestershire sauce
1 tablespoon flour
1 teaspoon tomato purée
150 ml (¼ pint) beef stock
1 × 225 g (8 oz) can baked beans
salt and pepper to taste
For the topping
750 g (1½ lb) potatoes, peeled and diced
25 g (1 oz) butter
50 ml (2 fl oz) hot milk
beaten egg or a little grated cheese to complete

Preparation time:	25 minutes
Cooking time:	32–35 minutes
Microwave setting:	High and conventional grill

Canned baked beans make minced beef go further, and add valuable fibre

—1—

Put the oil, onion and carrot in a large bowl. Cover and microwave for 3 minutes. Stir in the mince, then microwave for 5 minutes, stirring every 1½ minutes to break up the mince.

● With a little bit of guidance, older children can easily learn how to prepare and cook food. Unlike a conventional oven, a microwave heats only the food and not the oven itself, reducing the risk of accidental burns.
● Put out the correct cooking equipment for each recipe to avoid the child using metal dishes by mistake.
● Show children how to reheat individual portions.

—2—

Add the parsley, Worcestershire sauce, flour, purée, stock and beans, with a little seasoning. When well mixed, cover and microwave for 10 minutes, stirring after 5 minutes. Taste for seasoning, then spoon into a microwave-proof serving dish.

—3—

Put the potatoes into a large clean bowl with four tablespoons of water. Cover and microwave for 10–12 minutes until tender. Drain well, then mash until smooth with the butter and hot milk. Season to taste.

—4—

Spoon or pipe the potato over the mince. Microwave for 4–5 minutes to reheat then brush with beaten egg or sprinkle with cheese and flash under a hot grill until browned.

Fishy Macaroni Pie

Serves 6 to 8
275 g (10 oz) wholewheat macaroni
450 g (1 lb) smoked haddock fillet
300 ml (½ pint) milk
50 g (2 oz) butter or margarine
25 g (1 oz) flour
100 g (4 oz) grated cheese
2 hardboiled eggs, chopped
150 ml (¼ pint) soured cream
salt, pepper and cayenne to taste
For the topping
75 g (3 oz) wholemeal breadcrumbs
¼ teaspoon mustard powder
chopped parsley

Preparation time:	20 minutes
Cooking time:	28 minutes
Microwave setting:	High

Tasty smoked haddock turns every day macaroni cheese into a special family treat

—1—

Cook the macaroni on top of the stove, according to the packet directions. Drain and rinse with hot water.

—2—

Meanwhile, put the fish in a single layer in a microwave-proof dish. Pour over the milk, then cover and microwave for 8 minutes, or until the fish flakes easily. Remove the fish from the cooking liquid and flake the flesh, discarding the skin.

—3—

Put half the butter in a jug and microwave for 45 seconds. Stir in the flour and the cooking liquid from the fish. Microwave for 3 minutes, stirring every minute. Stir in the cheese. Microwave for 1 minute. Stir in the eggs, soured cream, fish and macaroni. Season to taste. Spoon into a microwave-proof serving dish.

—4—

Put the remaining butter (25 g/1 oz) in a bowl. Microwave for 30 seconds to melt. Stir in the breadcrumbs, mustard powder and a pinch of cayenne pepper. Mix well, then spoon this mixture on top of the fish macaroni. Microwave for 6 minutes until piping hot. Serve immediately.

Sea Bass Moroccan-Style

Serves 4

1 kg (2 lb) sea bass or mackerel
2 tablespoons soya or olive oil
1 tablespoon ground cumin
1 teaspoon paprika
1 clove garlic, crushed
2 shallots, finely sliced
grated rind of 1 lemon
2 tablespoons chopped fresh coriander or parsley
salt and pepper to taste
To garnish
coriander sprigs
lemon wedges

Preparation time:	10 minutes
Cooking time:	8–10 minutes
Microwave setting:	High

A simple but delicious dish that's sure to impress. Serve with a crisp salad

—1—

Clean the fish, trim fins and tail and scale if necessary. Rinse under cold running water and pat dry.

—2—

Combine all the remaining ingredients, spoon on top of the fish and rub in well. Put the fish in a large roasting bag, twisting the ends tightly and fastening with an elastic band.

—3—

Place on a plate and microwave for 8–10 minutes, depending on the thickness of the fish, until the flesh flakes easily.

—4—

Arrange the fish on a serving plate and spoon over all the juices that have collected in the bag.

—5—

Garnish with the coriander sprigs and lemon wedges. Serve immediately.

Tagliatelle Verde with Hot Pepper Sauce

Serves 4

275 g (10 oz) green tagliatelle
3 tablespoons olive oil
1 to 2 cloves garlic, crushed
1 large red pepper, cored and thinly sliced
1 × 400 g (14 oz) can plum tomatoes, drained and chopped
25 g (1 oz) black olives, stoned and sliced
salt, black pepper and tabasco to taste

Preparation time:	10 minutes
Cooking time:	10 minutes
Microwave setting:	High

Fresh tagliatelle verde (green noodles), found in the chilled cabinets of large supermarkets, are very quick to cook. Served with crusty wholemeal bread and cheese, this makes a good quick supper

—1—

Cook the pasta in plenty of boiling water, on top of the stove, according to the packet directions. Do not overcook – it should be *al dente* rather than very soft.

—2—

Drain, then toss in two tablespoons of the olive oil and plenty of black pepper.

—3—

While the pasta is cooking, prepare the sauce. Put all the remaining ingredients in a bowl. Microwave for 6 minutes, stirring every 2 minutes, until the sauce is thick.

—4—

Serve the pasta on warmed plates with the hot pepper sauce spooned on top.

Chicken and Prawn Saté with Peanut Sauce

Serves 6 as a first course

175 g (6 oz) boneless, skinless chicken breasts
175 g (6 oz) large, peeled
Mediterranean prawns

For the marinade
2 tablespoons soy sauce
1 tablespoon tomato ketchup
1 tablespoon marmalade

For the sauce
1 tablespoon soya oil
1 clove garlic (or to taste), crushed
25 g (1 oz) onion or spring
onion, finely chopped
4 tablespoons crunchy peanut butter
1 dried chilli, crushed
2 tablespoons soy sauce
3 tablespoons lemon juice
2 tablespoons clear honey
4 tablespoons coconut milk

To garnish
lemon wedges

Preparation time:	25 minutes plus marinating
Cooking time:	11–12 minutes
Microwave setting:	High

An unusual and delicious Indonesian dish, cooked on wooden skewers

—1—

Cut the chicken into strips about 5 mm by 5 cm (⅛ by 2 in).

—2—

Rinse the prawns and pat dry. If wished, make a small slit and remove the black vein that runs down the back of each prawn.

—3—

Mix the ingredients for the marinade with two tablespoons water. Add the chicken strips and prawns and toss well. Cover and leave to marinate for a couple of hours.

—4—

Drain and thread on to wooden skewers (reserve the marinade).

—5—

For the peanut sauce. Put the oil, garlic and onion into a bowl. Cover and microwave for 2 minutes.

—6—

Add all the remaining ingredients listed for the sauce and stir well. Microwave for 3 to 4 minutes, stirring after 1½ minutes, until the sauce has boiled and thickened. Set aside and keep warm.

—7—

Place the chicken and prawn skewers on the microwave rack. Microwave for 6 minutes, brushing with the reserved marinade every 2 minutes.

—8—

Serve immediately, garnished with lemon wedges and accompanied by the sauce.

Sea Bass Moroccan Style; Tagliatelle Verde with Hot Pepper Sauce; Chicken and Prawn Saté with Peanut Sauce

Savoury Glazed Leg of Lamb

Serves 4–6

1 × 1½ kg (3 lb) lean leg of lamb
2 tablespoons plain flour
2 tablespoons sage and onion flavoured mustard
1–2 tablespoons white wine
freshly ground black pepper
4 tablespoons redcurrant jelly
1 tablespoon lemon juice
2 tablespoons port

Preparation time:	20 minutes plus marinating
Cooking time:	35–40 minutes plus standing
Microwave setting:	High and Medium

Tender lamb is covered with a delicious, aromatic mustard and herb crust, then glazed with redcurrant jelly. Complement it with a rich gravy made from the meat juices and port

—1—

Trim all the excess fat from the lamb, then score the surface with the point of a sharp knife.

—2—

Make a paste of the flour, mustard, white wine and pepper and use to coat the lamb. Pierce the lamb all over with a skewer to help the flavours penetrate. Put into a deep dish and leave to marinate for 1–2 hours.

—3—

Microwave on high power for 15 minutes. Remove, and cover knuckle end with a small piece of foil (shiny side inside). Return to the microwave for 10–15 minutes on medium power (depending on the size of the joint and how you like your meat cooked). Remove.

—4—

Put the redcurrant jelly and lemon juice in a small bowl and microwave on medium power for 2 minutes until the mixture is bubbling. Pour over the lamb, basting well.

—5—

Return the lamb to the microwave and cook on high power for 6 minutes, basting every 2 minutes. Remove, cover loosely with foil and leave to stand for 10 minutes.

—6—

Tip the meat juices into a gravy boat. Stir in the port and a little seasoning. Microwave on medium power for 2 minutes and serve with the meat.

Braised Red Cabbage

Serves 6

1 large onion, thinly sliced
25 g (1 oz) butter or margarine
450 g (1 lb) finely shredded red cabbage
1 cooking apple, peeled, cored and diced
1 tablespoon brown sugar
65 ml (2½ fl oz) each red wine vinegar and hot water
2 tablespoons mint jelly (or redcurrant jelly)
salt and pepper to taste

Preparation time:	15 minutes plus draining and chilling
Cooking time:	29–34 minutes
Microwave setting:	High

Delicious served with roasted meat

—1—

Put the onion and butter or margarine in a large bowl. Cover and microwave for 2 minutes.

—2—

Meanwhile put the cabbage into a colander over the sink. Pour over a kettle of boiling water and leave to drain.

—3—

Uncover the bowl and stir in the drained cabbage, apple, sugar, vinegar, water and seasoning. Mix well, then cover with cling film and microwave for 25–30 minutes until the cabbage is tender, stirring occasionally.

—4—

Stir in the jelly, taste for seasoning, adding more salt, pepper, vinegar or sugar as necessary. Microwave for 2 minutes.

—5—

Stir well, then serve immediately or leave to cool, then cover and chill.

—6—

To reheat. Cook for 5–7 minutes, stirring occasionally until thoroughly hot (the time will depend on the size and shape of the dish, and how cold the cabbage is to begin with).

Hazelnut Sponge Puddings

Serves 6

75 g (3 oz) butter or margarine
120 g (4½ oz) caster sugar
grated rind of ½ lemon
65 ml (2½ fl oz) milk
175 g (6 oz) plain flour
3 teaspoons baking powder
75 g (3 oz) hazelnuts, roughly
chopped, and browned
3 egg whites
6 cups, greased and base-lined

Preparation time:	15 minutes
Cooking time:	6–7 minutes plus standing
Microwave setting:	High

Cook individual puddings in teacups (without gold rims), Pyrex glasses or paper cups for a light, tangy sweet that'll soon be a family favourite

—1—

Cream the butter or margarine with the sugar and lemon rind until soft and fluffy.

—2—

Stir in the milk, then flour sifted with the baking powder, and then the hazelnuts.

—3—

Whisk the egg whites until they form peaks and carefully fold into the mixture in three batches. Spoon into the prepared cups, then microwave for 6–7 minutes.

—4—

Leave to stand for 5–10 minutes, then turn out and serve the puddings with Mocha Sauce.

Mocha Sauce

50 g (2 oz) demerara sugar
2 teaspoons very strong black coffee
15 g (½ oz) butter or margarine
100 g (4 oz) plain chocolate

Preparation time:	5 minutes
Cooking time:	2½ minutes
Microwave setting:	High

Perfect with sponge puddings, ice cream, profiteroles or light, crisp meringues

—1—

Put the sugar, coffee, and 3 tablespoons of water into a jug. Microwave for 2½ minutes or until the mixture boils.

—2—

Add the butter or margarine and chocolate. Stir until melted and the sauce is smooth.

—3—

Serve immediately in the same jug or a warmed sauce boat.

Chunky Terrine

Serves 8–10

225 g (8 oz) rindless streaky bacon
15 g (½ oz) butter or margarine
1 onion, finely chopped
450 g (1 lb) pork, coarsely minced
225 g (8 oz) stewing veal, coarsely minced
225 g (8 oz) chicken livers, chopped
1 clove garlic, peeled and crushed
¼ teaspoon allspice
¼ teaspoon ground cloves
¼ teaspoon ground nutmeg
salt and pepper to taste
150 ml (¼ pint) double cream
2 tablespoons brandy (optional)
1 gammon steak, about 150 g (5 oz)
1 bay leaf
1 × 1.75 litre (3 pint) Pyrex or
microwave-ware loaf pan or terrine

Preparation time:	35 minutes plus chilling
Cooking time:	49–55 minutes
Microwave setting:	High, then Defrost

An excellent starter that can also be served as a light lunch with fresh, crusty French bread and a crispy green salad

—1—

Stretch the bacon rashers with the back of a knife and use to line the terrine, reserving a few for the top.

—2—

Put the butter in a small basin, then microwave on high power for 1–2 minutes until frothy. Add the onion and microwave on high power for 3 minutes to soften. Leave to cool for a few minutes.

—3—

In a large bowl, mix the cooled onion with the pork, veal, chicken livers, garlic, spices, seasonings, cream and brandy.

—4—

Cut the gammon into strips about 5 mm (¼ in) thick. Spread a third of the meat mixture in the lined terrine and smooth the surface. Arrange a layer of half the gammon strips on top, then a layer of the meat mixture. Cover with the remaining gammon strips, then finish with a layer of the remaining meat mixture. Smooth the top and cover with the reserved bacon slices. Place the bay leaf on top, then cover the terrine with cling film.

—5—

Cook in the microwave on defrost for 45–50 minutes. Remove from microwave and leave to cool.

—6—

Put a weighted saucer or small plate on top of the terrine and chill overnight. Turn out and serve, thickly sliced, with wholewheat bread.

Moussaka

Serves 6

450 g (1 lb) medium aubergines, sliced
2 medium onions, finely chopped
1 tablespoon soya oil
1 × 400 g (14 oz) can tomatoes
750 g (1½ lb) good quality minced beef
1½ beef stock cubes
a sprinkling of dried herbs to taste
salt and pepper to taste
40 g (1½ oz) butter or margarine
40 g (½ oz) flour
450 ml (15 fl oz) milk
1 egg
100 g (4 oz) strong Cheddar cheese, grated
1 × 2.25 litre (4 pint) oblong
microwave-proof dish, greased

Preparation time:	20 minutes plus standing
Cooking time:	27–29 minutes
Microwave setting:	High

A quick and tasy supper dish that's always a firm favourite and it freezes well, too

—1—

Sprinkle the aubergines with a little salt, leave for 15 minutes, then rinse with cold water and pat dry.

—2—

Mix the chopped onions with the oil and aubergines. Cover with cling film and microwave for 7 minutes. Stir in the drained tomatoes, cover and microwave for 1 minute. Set aside, covered.

—3—

Mix the meat with the stock cubes, herbs, two tablespoons of hot water, and a little seasoning. Cover with cling film. Microwave for 6 minutes, stirring after 3 minutes.

—4—

Put the butter or margarine, flour and milk into a jug, microwave for 5 minutes, stirring occasionally. Beat in the egg and stir in all but 1 tablespoon of the grated cheese after 4 minutes.

—5—

Layer up the vegetables, meat and cheese sauce in the greased dish, finishing with sauce. Sprinkle with the remaining cheese. Microwave for 8–10 minutes.

Monster Salad

1 Cos lettuce or Chinese leaves
1 bunch watercress
4 spring onions
150 ml (¼ pint) French dressing

Preparation time: 5 minutes

Croutons can be added to the salad for extra crunch

—1—

Rinse and shred the lettuce or Chinese leaves. Pick over the watercress, and slice the spring onions thinly.

—2—

Put into a salad bowl. Pour over the dressing and toss well. Serve as soon as possible.

Jacket Potatoes

Serves 8
8 large baking potatoes, scrubbed
100 g (4 oz) butter or margarine, or flavoured butter
or 225 g (8 oz) cottage cheese with chives
or 225 g (8 oz) grated
Cheddar cheese

Preparation time: 5 minutes
Cooking time: 40 minutes
Microwave setting: High

Serve with butter, flavoured with chopped herbs and crushed garlic, cottage cheese or grated Cheddar cheese

—1—

Pierce the potatoes all over with a sharp fork. Microwave for 5–6 minutes per potato (all 8 potatoes will take about 40 minutes).

—2—

Split and fill with chosen filling.

Moussaka; Monster Salad; Chunky Terrine; Jacket Potatoes, served with cottage cheese with chives; Special Chocolate Mousse (p 62)

Special Chocolate Mousse

Serves 6

90 g (3½ oz) unsalted butter
4 level tablespoons caster sugar
4 eggs, separated
225 g (8 oz) plain chocolate

Preparation time:	15 minutes plus chilling
Cooking time:	2½ minutes
Microwave setting:	High, then Medium

Serve in pretty glasses, or in coffee cups set on saucers, decorated with finely grated chocolate or a swirl of cream

—1—

Put the butter into a medium-sized bowl. Microwave on high power for 30 seconds.

—2—

Add the sugar and beat until light and fluffy. Gradually beat in the egg yolks.

—3—

Break up the chocolate. Put into a small bowl with 4 tablespoons water. Microwave on medium power for 2 minutes.

—4—

Beat the chocolate into the butter mixture, beating for 5 minutes or until the mixture is light and fluffy. Whisk the egg whites and fold in. Spoon into glasses or little cups or ramekins and chill until firm. Decorate as wished; serve chilled.

● To ensure even cooking it is important that portions of poultry or meat should be arranged so the thicker areas face in towards the centre of the microwave.
● To clean your microwave, a wipe with a soft cloth rinsed in a mild detergent should be sufficient – do not use scourers.
● 100 g (4 oz) chocolate can be melted in a bowl for 2 minutes on 'high'.
● Crisp up stale biscuits for 20 seconds on high.

Smoked Haddock Omelette

Serves 4

750 g (1½ lb) smoked haddock fillet
300 ml (½ pint) milk
25 g (1 oz) unsalted butter
6 eggs, size 3
salt and pepper to taste
50 g (2 oz) Cheddar or
Gruyère cheese, grated
150 ml (¼ pint) double cream,
lightly whipped

Preparation time:	20 minutes
Cooking time:	10 minutes
Microwave setting:	High and conventional grill

A speedy supper dish using tasty smoked haddock – choose undyed fish if possible

—1—

Arrange the fish fillets in a single layer in a shallow dish. Pour over the milk, and dot with a little of the butter.

—2—

Microwave for 5 minutes or until the fish flakes easily. Lift the fish out of the liquid, and flake into a bowl, discarding the skin. Beat the eggs with one tablespoon of the fish poaching liquid, and a little seasoning. Stir in the fish and half the grated cheese.

—3—

Put the remaining butter in a 23 cm (9 in) round shallow dish. Microwave for 2 minutes until the butter is melted and hot. Pour in the egg mixture and microwave for 2 minutes. After 1 minute, gently draw the cooked egg away from the edges so that the uncooked egg runs into its place.

—4—

Put the dish under a heated grill for a few moments so the mixture puffs up and sets. Spread the whipped cream on top and sprinkle with the remaining cheese. Flash under the grill until golden and bubbling. Cut into four and serve immediately.

Chicken Gumbo

Serves 6 to 8
6 chicken joints
4 tablespoons soya oil
225 g (8 oz) okra, washed and trimmed
1 bacon chop or gammon steak,
about 225 g (8 oz), cubed
1 large onion, chopped
1 stick celery, sliced
2 cloves garlic, crushed
1 each small red, green and yellow pepper, cored
and diced
1 tablespoon tomato purée
2 × 400 g (14 oz) cans tomatoes, drained and
chopped
a large bouquet garni
salt and cayenne pepper to taste
To complete
chopped fresh parsley

Preparation time:	20 minutes
Cooking time:	40 minutes
Microwave setting:	High and conventional hob

An attractive and richly-flavoured dish from Louisiana, in the south of the United States. Serve with plainly cooked rice

—1—

Quickly brown the chicken in the hot oil on top of the stove. Drain and put in a large microwave-proof casserole.

—2—

Fry the okra in the same oil for a few seconds, lift out, draining well, and set aside.

—3—

Fry the cubed bacon, onion, celery and garlic in the oil until golden. Add to the casserole with all the remaining ingredients, except the okra. Mix well, then cover and microwave for 25 minutes, stirring twice during the cooking time.

—4—

Add the okra. Cover and microwave for a further 5 minutes or until the chicken is cooked and tender, and the okra is soft.

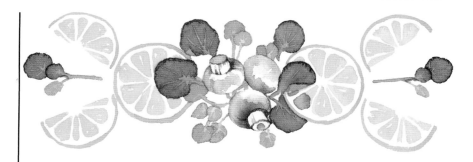

(The exact time will depend on size of chicken pieces and the dish.)

—5—

Taste and adjust the seasonings as necessary. Sprinkle with chopped parsley and serve.

Tipsy Bananas

Serves 6
8 bananas
grated rind and juice of 2 lemons
300 ml (½ pint) sweet cider
8 tablespoons soft brown sugar
1 teaspoon grated nutmeg
¼ teaspoon ground cinnamon
vanilla ice cream

Preparation time:	5 minutes
Cooking time:	7–9 minutes
Microwave setting:	High

Nothing could be simpler than this dish of bananas baked in sweet cider and spices, and you can serve it either hot or cold

—1—

Peel the bananas. Halve and toss in the lemon juice to prevent browning. Put into a baking dish.

—2—

Mix the cider with the lemon rind, sugar and spices in a jug. Microwave for 1 minute.

—3—

Pour the mixture over the bananas and microwave for 6–8 minutes until heated through. Serve hot or cold with ice cream.

Delicious meat-free meals

VEGETARIAN SPECIALS

You don't have to be vegetarian to enjoy the occasional meat-free meal, and whether you are committed, or simply experimenting with vegetarian dishes, you'll find this selection of recipes a useful addition to your range of choices. Using a microwave is by far the best way to cook vegetables. The results are equally impressive with both simple vegetable dishes and our more adventurous recipes. This is because microwaved vegetables retain their shape, colour, flavour and texture more readily than with conventional cooking methods.

Flageolet and Leek Soup

Serves 4 to 6

4 medium leeks, washed and thinly sliced
1 large potato, peeled and diced
25 g (1 oz) butter or margarine
1 bouquet garni
salt and pepper to taste
900 ml (1½ pints) boiling vegetable stock
1 × 400 g (14 oz) can flageolet beans
2 tablespoons chopped fresh parsley

Preparation time:	10 minutes
Cooking time:	25 minutes plus standing
Microwave setting:	High

A chunky, wholesome soup that's a meal in itself when served with some good bread and cheese

—1—

Put the leeks and potato into a bowl with the butter. Cover and microwave for 10 minutes, stirring once.

—2—

Add the bouquet garni, seasoning, stock and drained beans. Cover and microwave for 15 minutes, or until the beans are tender. Leave to stand for 10 minutes.

—3—

Remove the bouquet garni. Taste and adjust the seasoning as necessary. Sprinkle with parsley and serve with wholemeal bread.

Sweet and Sour Okra

Serves 4 to 6

450 g (1 lb) okra
3 tablespoons soya oil
½ teaspoon ground turmeric
1 teaspoon ground cumin
2 teaspoons ground coriander
1 green chilli, seeded and
finely chopped
2 cloves garlic (or to taste), crushed
65 ml (2½ fl oz) vegetable stock
salt to taste
1 teaspoon brown sugar
grated rind of 1 lime
1 tablespoon lime juice
1 tablespoon chopped fresh coriander

Preparation time:	5 minutes
Cooking time:	6–8 minutes
Microwave setting:	High

Choose small, bright green, young okra as larger, older okra tend to be woody

—1—

Thoroughly wash and dry the okra. Trim the stem end.

—2—

Heat the oil in a frying pan on top of the stove. Fry the okra over high heat for 1 minute, then dry in kitchen paper.

—3—

Put into a microwave-proof dish with the remaining ingredients (except the fresh coriander). Cover and microwave for 6–8 minutes until tender.

—4—

Taste for seasoning. Garnish with fresh coriander and serve immediately.

● You don't have to be a vegetarian to enjoy these appealing recipes – a lunch or supper that excludes meat can be wholesome and delicious.
● If a member of your family is vegetarian, you probably already buy free-range eggs and vegetarian or rennet-free cheese (for lacto-vegetarians) and stock such staples as brown rice, pulses and beans. Vegetarian food can be delicious enough to tempt everyone – Rich Vegetable Curry and Savoury Potatoes will soon be firm family favourites.
● We've also included a few recipes useful for keen vegetable growers, to use up all those leeks, onions, tomatoes and courgettes. Use these recipes too to take advantage of a seasonal glut. Make Cheesy Stuffed Peppers, for example, when peppers are cheap, freeze after stuffing, then heat in the microwave straight from the freezer.

Cheesy Stuffed Peppers

Serves 4

4 medium peppers
2 tablespoons oil
1 large onion, finely chopped
4 sticks celery, chopped
350 g (12 oz) tomatoes, skinned
1 tablespoon tomato purée
1 clove garlic, crushed
2 teaspoons chopped fresh basil
¼ teaspoon ground cinnamon
salt and pepper to taste
75 g (3 oz) cheese, diced
50 g (2 oz) seedless raisins
75 g (3 oz) nuts (pinenuts, hazelnuts, almonds or a mixture)
175 g (6 oz) cooked brown rice

Preparation time: 15 minutes
Cooking time: 19–23 minutes
Microwave setting: High

Choose red, green or yellow peppers and fill with this fluffy rice stuffing. A colourful and flavourful meal that's full of goodness – and with the added surprise of crunchy nuts

—1—

Carefully remove the core and seeds from each pepper. Put into a bowl of boiling salted water. Microwave for 3 minutes. Lift out the peppers and drain thoroughly.

—2—

Put the oil, onion and celery into another bowl. Cover with cling film and microwave for 2–3 minutes, until tender.

—3—

Chop the tomatoes and add to the onion mixture with the tomato purée, garlic, basil and seasoning. Microwave for 4–5 minutes until thick. Stir in remaining ingredients. Taste for seasoning.

—4—

Divide the mixture between the peppers, stand the filled peppers upright in a soufflé dish. Microwave for 10–12 minutes until thoroughly hot.

Fresh Tomato Soup

Serves 4

2 medium onions, peeled and finely chopped
2 small green chillis, seeded and chopped
2 cloves garlic, peeled and crushed
1.5 litres (2½ pts) tomato juice
salt and pepper to taste
1¾ kg (4 lb) ripe tomatoes
celery tops to garnish (optional)

Preparation time: 20 minutes
Cooking time: 30–35 minutes
Microwave setting: Medium

How to make good use of a glut of home-grown tomatoes. This spicy and nutritious soup will freeze very well, too

—1—

Mix the onions and chillis with the garlic and stir into half the tomato juice with a little seasoning in a non-metallic mixing bowl. Cover with cling film and microwave for 12–15 minutes until the onions are very soft.

—2—

Meanwhile, put the tomatoes into boiling water for 10 seconds, then place immediately in a bowl of cold water. Drain and peel off the skins. (This can also be done in a microwave, but is time-consuming.) Halve the tomatoes, and carefully remove the seeds. Roughly chop the flesh, reserving as much of the tomatoes' juice as possible.

—3—

Add the chopped tomatoes, with their juice, and the remaining tomato juice, to the onion mixture. Microwave for 18–20 minutes. Liquidize or purée in a mouli sieve.

—4—

Taste for seasoning. Serve hot or cold garnished with celery tops and accompanied by crunchy bread rolls.

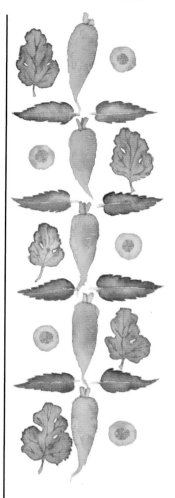

Chick Pea Vegetable Goulash

Serves 4 to 6
3 tablespoons olive oil
1 medium onion, thinly sliced
2 medium carrots, peeled and thinly sliced
2 medium courgettes, wiped and thinly sliced
175 g (6 oz) white cabbage, shredded
2 tomatoes, skinned and chopped
1 × 400 g (14 oz) can chick peas, drained
1½ tablespoons paprika, or to taste
1 teaspoon mixed dried herbs
600 ml (1 pint) tomato juice
salt and pepper to taste

Preparation time:	10 minutes
Cooking time:	21 minutes
Microwave setting:	High

The vegetables can be quickly sliced and shredded in a processor. Serve this tasty vegetable casserole with brown rice, noodles or boiled potatoes

—1—

Put the oil, onion and carrot in a bowl or microwave casserole dish. Cover and microwave for 5 minutes.

—2—

Stir in the courgettes, cabbage and chopped tomato. Cover and microwave for 6 minutes, stirring twice during the cooking time.

—3—

Stir in the chick peas, paprika, herbs, tomato juice and a little seasoning.

—4—

Cover and microwave for 10 minutes or until the vegetables are tender. Taste for seasoning and adjust if wished. Serve immediately.

Tomato Ring, Filled with Green Beans and Peppers

Serves 6 as first course, 4 as main dish
2 × 400 g (14 oz) cans plum tomatoes
a strip of lemon rind
1 clove garlic (or to taste), crushed
6 peppercorns
1 bay leaf
1½ teaspoons Gelozone
vegetable gel powder or
1 tablespoon powdered gelatine
2 tablespoons sherry (or to taste)
sugar, salt and pepper to taste
For the filling
100 g (4 oz) French beans, topped and tailed
½ each small red and yellow
pepper, cored and sliced
2 tablespoons French dressing
1 × 600 ml (1 pint) ring mould

Preparation time:	20 minutes plus chilling
Cooking time:	12–13 minutes
Microwave setting:	High

A lovely summer first course that's elegant enough for a party buffet table

—1—

Roughly chop the tomatoes. Place in a large bowl with their liquid, the lemon rind, garlic, peppercorns and bay leaf.

—2—

Cover and microwave for 8 minutes. Remove the peppercorns and bay leaf, then sieve. Whisk the Gelozone and sherry into the hot liquid *or*, if using gelatine, sprinkle the gelatine over the sherry in a small bowl. Leave to soak for 5 minutes, then microwave for 1–2 minutes until melted. Cool slightly, then stir into the tomato purée.

—3—

Stir in sugar and seasonings to taste. Pour into the dampened ring mould and chill overnight or until set.

—4—

For the filling. Put the beans into a bowl with two tablespoons water. Microwave for 3 minutes.

—5—

Rinse with cold water, then drain thoroughly. Mix the beans with the peppers and toss in the dressing. Chill until ready to serve.

—6—

Turn out the ring mould on to a serving plate and fill the centre with the salad. Serve immediately.

Stuffed Vine Leaves

Serves 4 to 6

28 vine leaves
2 tablespoons olive oil
4 spring onions, finely chopped
2 tomatoes, skinned and chopped
1 tablespoon fresh mint or coriander, chopped
1 clove garlic crushed
1 stick celery, finely chopped
¼ teaspoon each ground cinnamon and allspice
a pinch of ground turmeric
juice of 1 lemon
salt and pepper to taste
175 g (6 oz) cooked brown rice
50 g (2 oz) pine nuts
150 ml (¼ pint) vegetable stock

Preparation time:	15 minutes
Cooking time:	24 minutes
Microwave setting:	High, then Medium

Spicy rice and pine nuts make a good stuffing for vine leaves. Serve hot or cold

—1—

Thoroughly rinse the vine leaves in hot water. Drain.

—2—

Put the oil, onions, tomatoes, mint (or coriander), garlic, celery and spices in a large bowl. Cover and microwave on high power for 4 minutes, stirring once during the cooking time.

—3—

Stir in the lemon juice, seasoning, rice and pine nuts. Use the mixture to fill the vine leaves. To do this, place a leaf vein-side up on a work surface. Put a tablespoon of filling in the centre. Fold in the stem end, then both sides, and roll up to make a neat parcel.

—4—

Tightly pack the stuffed leaves into an oiled shallow dish, so they form a neat, single layer. Pour over the vetegable stock. Microwave on medium power for 20 minutes. Serve hot or cold.

Tomato Ring, filled with Green Beans and Peppers; Chick Pea Vegetable Goulash; Stuffed Vine Leaves

Broccoli and Hazelnut Canneloni

Serves 4

450 g (1 lb) broccoli, cut into florets
1 tablespoon olive oil
1 medium onion, finely chopped
1 clove garlic (or to taste), crushed
100 g (4 oz) cottage cheese
2 teaspoons toasted sesame seeds
25 g (1 oz) hazelnuts, roughly chopped and toasted
salt and pepper
8 canneloni tubes
150 ml (¼ pint) soured cream
4 tablespoons single cream
50 g (2 oz) freshly grated Parmesan cheese

Preparation time:	10 minutes
Cooking time:	15–20 minutes
Microwave setting:	High and conventional grill

Almost any nuts can be used in place of the hazelnuts, if wished

—1—

Put the broccoli florets into a bowl with two tablespoons water. Cover and microwave for 3 minutes.

—2—

Put the oil, onion and garlic in another bowl. Cover and microwave for 3 minutes or until softened. Stir in the broccoli, cottage cheese, sesame seeds, nuts and season to taste.

—3—

Meanwhile, cook the canneloni in plenty of boiling water, on top of the stove, according to the directions on the packet.

—4—

Fill the canneloni with the stuffing and arrange in a greased, shallow microwave-proof serving dish. Mix the soured cream with the single cream and Parmesan. Spoon over the pasta. When ready to serve, microwave for 7 minutes or until thoroughly heated. Flash under a heated grill to brown.

Mushroom-Stuffed Artichokes

Serves 2

2 medium size globe artichokes
5 tablespoons lemon juice
½ medium onion, chopped
50 g (2 oz) button mushrooms, chopped
15 g (½ oz) butter
40 g (1½ oz) fresh brown breadcrumbs
1 clove garlic, crushed
2 small tomatoes, skinned, seeded and chopped
2 teaspoons chopped chives
25 g (1 oz) walnuts, roughly chopped
salt and pepper to taste

Preparation time:	20 minutes plus soaking
Cooking time:	23–25 minutes
Microwave setting:	High

The microwave oven really comes into its own when cooking globe artichokes – no more large pans of boiling water dominating the kitchen, and far reduced cooking time

—1—

Using a large, heavy, sharp knife, cut off the artichoke stalks and the two lower rows of leaves to form a flat base. Using a pair of kitchen scissors, snip off the leaf tips. Stand upside down in a large bowl of cold water with two tablespoons lemon juice added. Leave for an hour, then drain.

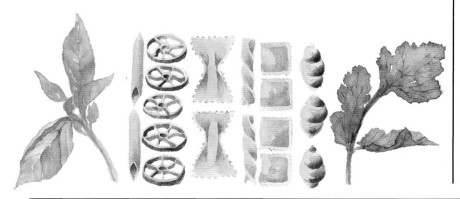

—2—

Place in a roasting bag with the remaining three tablespoons lemon juice and four tablespoons water. Seal with string or an elastic band. Microwave for 15–16 minutes until the leaves pull away easily.

—3—

While the artichokes are cooking, prepare the stuffing. Put the onion, mushrooms and butter in a bowl and microwave for 3 minutes, stirring halfway through. Stir in the remaining ingredients and season to taste. Microwave for 3 minutes.

—4—

To stuff artichokes, carefully separate the leaves and pull out the central leaves to expose the hairy choke. Using a sharp-pointed teaspoon, carefully remove the choke, taking care not to damage the artichoke bottom.

—5—

Spoon the stuffing into the artichoke and microwave for 2–3 minutes until heated through. Serve with crusty bread, and garlic or lemon mayonnaise.

Hot Fennel with Cream Cheese Sauce

Serves 6
2 large heads fennel
salt and pepper to taste
½ teaspoon oregano
½ medium onion, finely chopped
50 ml (2 fl oz) milk
50 g (2 oz) butter or margarine
50 g (2 oz) cream cheese

Preparation time: 5 minutes
Cooking time: 10–15 minutes
Microwave setting: High

An unusual yet easy vegetable accompaniment or first course

—1—

Slice the fennel into bite-sized pieces, rinse, then put into a microwave dish. Sprinkle with salt and pepper, the oregano and the onion.

—2—

Pour over the milk. Dot with the butter and cream cheese. Microwave for 10–15 minutes until tender. Toss gently before serving.

Eve's Pudding

Serves 4 to 6
450 g (1 lb) cooking apples
50 g (2 oz) raisins
4 cloves
50 g (2 oz) caster sugar
finely grated rind of ½ lemon
For the sponge topping
75 g (3 oz) soft margarine
75 g (3 oz) caster sugar
1 egg
100 g (4 oz) self-raising flour, sifted
pinch of ground cinnamon
4 tablespoons milk
1 × 1.5 litre (2½ pint) microwave-proof dish, buttered

Preparation time: 10 minutes
Cooking time: 7–8 minutes
Microwave setting: High

—1—

Peel, core and slice the apples and place in the dish with the raisins, cloves, caster sugar and lemon rind. Cover and microwave on high power for 2 minutes.

—2—

Place the sponge topping ingredients together in a large bowl and beat until smooth. Spoon over the apple slices and spread evenly to completely cover.

—3—

Cover and microwave for 5–6 minutes until well risen. Stand for 3 minutes.

Rich Vegetable Curry

Serves 4 to 6

225 g (8 oz) okra, washed and trimmed
3 tablespoons soya oil
1 medium onion, finely chopped
1 green chilli, cored and seeded
1 × 2½ cm (1 in) piece fresh root ginger, peeled
2 cloves garlic, peeled
½ teaspoon salt, or to taste
½ teaspoon ground cumin
1 teaspoon turmeric
1 teaspoon garam masala
1 × 400 g (14 oz) can tomatoes, drained
2 medium potatoes, peeled and cubed
1 medium aubergine, washed,
trimmed and cubed
100 g (4 oz) cauliflower florets, washed
150 ml (¼ pint) boiling vegetable stock or water
100 g (4 oz) roasted cashews

Preparation time:	20 minutes
Cooking time:	16–20 minutes
Microwave setting:	High

Add more nuts to this colourful spicy curry for extra protein and serve with brown rice. Omit the chilli if you prefer a milder flavour

Pat the okra dry on kitchen paper towels. Heat half the oil in a frying pan and quickly fry the okra. Set aside.

—2—

Put the remaining oil and onion into a large bowl. Microwave for 1 minute.

—3—

Finely chop the chilli with the ginger and garlic. Stir into the onion with the salt and spices. Microwave for 1 minute.

—4—

Stir in the tomatoes, potatoes and aubergines. Cover with pierced cling film and microwave for 8–10 minutes until almost tender.

—5—

Stir well, then add the cauliflower, okra and stock. Cover with cling film and microwave for 6–8 minutes or until the vegetables are tender.

Banana and Carrot Cake; Rich Vegetable Curry; Egg and Tomato Crumble

—6—

Taste for seasoning and adjust as necessary. Stir in the cashew nuts and serve immediately.

Egg and Tomato Crumble

Serves 4
1 small onion, finely chopped
50 g (2 oz) butter or margarine
3 hard-boiled eggs, chopped
225 g (8 oz) tomatoes, skinned
salt, pepper and cayenne to taste
75 g (3 oz) fresh wholemeal breadcrumbs
¼ teaspoon mustard powder
½ tablespoon chopped parsley
4 microwave-poof ramekins, buttered

Preparation time:	10 minutes
Cooking time:	10½ minutes
Microwave setting:	High

A quick, colourful supper dish

—1—

Put the onion and half the butter into a small bowl. Microwave for 4 minutes.

—2—

Quarter the tomatoes, discard the seeds, and roughly chop the flesh.

—3—

Layer up the onions, eggs and tomatoes in the ramekins, seasoning between each layer.

—4—

Melt the remaining butter in a bowl for 30 seconds. Stir in the breadcrumbs, a little cayenne and the mustard powder.

—5—

Divide the mixture between the ramekins. Microwave for 6 minutes. Sprinkle with parsley and serve immediately.

Banana and Carrot Cake

Makes two 18 cm (7 in) cakes
1 teaspoon ground mixed spice
2 teaspoons baking powder
250 g (9 oz) wholemeal flour
150 g (5 oz) soft, light brown sugar
2 ripe bananas, mashed
175 g (6 oz) carrots, grated
50 g (2 oz) California raisins
3 eggs, beaten
200 ml (7 fl oz) sunflower or soya oil
1.25 litre (2 pints) microwave-proof
ring moulds
For the icing
100 g (4 oz) icing sugar, sieved
1–2 tablespoons orange juice
grated rind of ½ orange

Preparation time:	15 minutes
Cooking time:	8 minutes
Microwave setting:	High

A deliciously moist cake – scrumptious and full of good things – and it couldn't be easier to make

—1—

Mix the spice, baking powder and flour in a large bowl. Stir in remaining ingredients, then beat until thoroughly blended.

—2—

Spoon into the mould. Microwave for 8 minutes, then turn out and leave to cool.

—3—

To make the icing: Mix the icing sugar with orange juice and rind until smooth. Drizzle over the cakes.

● Use greaseproof paper or kitchen paper towels to cover food which may splutter or pop during cooking, such as baked beans and chicken pieces. To prevent the paper flapping about in the microwave, secure it to the food with a cocktail stick. Otherwise you can tuck the ends of the paper under the dish (taking care the paper doesn't catch alight).

● Don't salt vegetables before cooking, as this can prolong the cooking time and cause them to dehydrate.

● To make perfect garlic bread, cut a French stick or baguette into 6 to 8 pieces. Microwave 60 g (2 oz) unsalted butter on high for 30 seconds. Beat in a crushed clove of garlic or a little garlic purée, and some finely chopped fresh herbs if wished.

Spread the butter over both sides of each piece of bread. Wrap in greaseproof paper and stand on a plate. Microwave on high for 2 minutes to heat through completely.

● The microwave is portable enough for patio entertaining and barbecues; it's useful for keeping food hot, partially cooking or reheating when entertaining outside.

A wonderful combination of tomatoes, mozzarella, pine kernels and aubergines flavoured with spice, herbs and garlic. Try serving it with brown rice

Italian-Style Baked Aubergine

Serves 3 to 4

3 medium aubergines
2 tablespoons olive oil
1 large onion, finely chopped
1 to 2 cloves garlic, crushed
1 × 400 g (14 oz) can tomatoes, drained and chopped
1 tablespoon tomato purée
2 tablespoons chopped parsley
1 teaspoon ground cinnamon
a pinch of caster sugar
2 tablespoons pine kernels
salt and pepper to taste
50 g (2 oz) mozzarella, thinly sliced

Preparation time:	20 minutes plus draining
Cooking time:	15½–16½ minutes
Microwave setting:	High

—1—

Trim the stems off the aubergines and cut in half lengthways. Sprinkle the cut edges with a little salt and leave to drain for 30 minutes.

—2—

Rinse with cold water and pat dry on kitchen paper towels.

—3—

Leaving the skins intact, scoop out the flesh and dice. Set aside. Brush the outside of the shells with a little of the olive oil.

—4—

Put into a shallow dish, cover with cling film and microwave for 4–5 minutes. Leave to stand while preparing stuffing.

—5—

Put the onion and garlic into a bowl with a tablespoon of olive oil. Cover with cling film and microwave for 2 minutes.

—6—

Add the diced aubergine flesh and tomatoes. Cover with cling film and microwave for 5 minutes.

—7—

Add all the remaining ingredients (except mozzarella). Stir well, then cover and microwave for 3 minutes.

—8—

Taste the stuffing, and adjust the seasonings as necessary. Spoon into the aubergine shells.

—9—

Top with the cheese and microwave for 1½ minutes until the dish is piping hot.

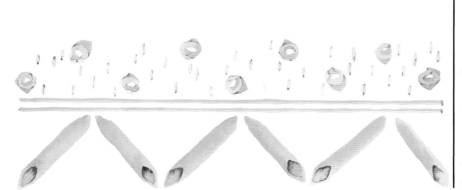

Savoury Potatoes

Serves 4

750 g (½ lb) large potatoes, peeled, cut in 1 cm (1 in) cubes
2 tablespoons soya oil
1 large clove garlic, crushed
2 teaspoons wholegrain mustard
½ teaspoon turmeric
1 teaspoon chilli powder
a large pinch ground coriander
salt to taste
4 eggs
To garnish
chopped fresh coriander, parsley or chives

Preparation time:	10 minutes
Cooking time:	15–20 minutes
Microwave setting:	High

This makes an unusual supper dish served with a big salad. For more 'heat' add extra chilli powder or a chopped chilli

—1—

Put the oil into a large bowl. Microwave for 2 minutes.

—2—

Stir in the garlic and mustard. Microwave for 1 minute.

—3—

Mix in the potatoes, turmeric and chilli powder, ground coriander and salt until each potato is thoroughly coated in the spicy mixture.

—4—

Cover with pierced cling film and microwave for 10–15 minutes, stirring occasionally, until the potatoes are cooked.

—5—

Spoon the potato mixture into a gratin dish and make four hollows. Break an egg into each hollow and pierce yolks with a cocktail stick.

—6—

Microwave for 2 minutes or until the eggs are just set, then garnish and serve.

Mushrooms à la Grècque

Serves 4

450 g (1 lb) button mushrooms
2 tablespoons olive oil
1 medium onion, finely chopped
1 clove garlic, crushed
225 g (8 oz) tomatoes, skinned and finely chopped
1 tablespoon tomato purée
1 tablespoon brown sugar
1 tablespoon fresh basil
½ teaspoon ground cumin
50 ml (2 fl oz) white wine
salt, pepper and cayenne to taste
To garnish
1 tablespoon chopped parsley

Preparation time:	5 minutes plus chilling
Cooking time:	6–8 minutes
Microwave setting:	High

This classic cold dish makes the perfect lunch on a warm day

—1—

Wipe the mushrooms and trim the stalks if necessary. Set aside.

—2—

Put all the remaining ingredients (except for garnish) into a large bowl. Cover with cling film and microwave for 3–4 minutes, stirring occasionally.

—3—

Stir in the mushrooms and taste for seasoning. Cover and microwave for 3–4 minutes until the mushrooms are tender.

—4—

Leave to cool then cover and chill before serving.

Vegetable Lasagne

Serves 4
1 medium onion, chopped
1 clove garlic, crushed
50 g (2 oz) butter or margarine
2 red peppers, cored and sliced
225 g (8 oz) mushrooms, sliced
1 medium cauliflower, broken into tiny florets
40 g (1½ oz) plain flour
300 ml (½ pint) milk
salt, cayenne and mustard powder to taste
175 g (6 oz) green lasagne
100 g (4 oz) grated cheese
2 tablespoons wholemeal breadcrumbs
2 tablespoons Parmesan cheese (optional)

Preparation time:	20 minutes
Cooking time:	30–33 minutes
Microwave setting:	High and conventional grill

For speed, and ease, choose the type of lasagne that doesn't need to be pre-cooked

—1—

Put the onion, garlic and 15 g (½ oz) butter into a bowl. Cover with cling film and microwave for 4 minutes. Add the peppers. Cover and microwave for 4 to 5 minutes until tender. Add the mushrooms and cauliflower florets. Cover and microwave for 5 minutes.

—2—

Put the remaining butter into a jug with the flour. Microwave for 1 minute. Whisk in milk, seasoning to taste and the grated cheese. Microwave for 6 minutes, whisking every 2 minutes.

—3—

Layer up the lasagne, vegetables and sauce in a gratin dish, finishing with a layer of cheese sauce. Microwave for 10–12 minutes, until bubbling and the lasagne is cooked. Sprinkle with breadcrumbs and Parmesan and brown under a hot grill.

Chinese-Style Rice with Egg

Serves 4
1 × 1 cm (½ in) piece fresh
ginger, finely chopped
1 clove garlic (or to taste), crushed
6 spring onions, chopped
2 tablespoons soya oil
25 g (1 oz) Chinese dried mushrooms, soaked and sliced
50 g (2 oz) water chestnuts, shredded
1 red pepper, cored and shredded
3 tablespoons vegetable stock
100 g (4 oz) bean sprouts, well washed
225 g (8 oz) cooked rice (brown or white)
1 teaspoon sesame oil
2 large eggs, beaten
salt and pepper to taste
To garnish
spring onion curls

Preparation time:	15 minutes
Cooking time:	12–16 minutes
Microwave setting:	High

A really attractive and nutritious rice dish, perfect with stir-fried vegetables, stuffed pancakes or spring rolls. Chinese dried mushrooms are available from speciality shops and large quality supermarkets

—1—

Put the ginger, garlic and spring onions into a large bowl with the oil and a little seasoning. Cover with cling film and microwave for 4–5 minutes.

—2—

Stir in the mushrooms, chestnuts, red pepper and stock. Cover with cling film and microwave for 3 minutes.

—3—

Stir in the bean sprouts and rice, then sprinkle over the sesame oil. Microwave for 4–7 minutes until piping hot (exact time will depend on the type of rice and its temperature).

x
y

—4—

Stir the beaten eggs gently into the rice mixture then microwave for 1 minute. Stir gently, taste for seasoning then serve garnished with onion curls.

Stuffed Cabbage and Tomato Bake

Serves 4

8 large cabbage leaves, rinsed

For the stuffing

1 tablespoon soya oil

2 sticks celery, chopped

1 medium onion, finely chopped

2 tomatoes, peeled, seeded and chopped

100 g (4 oz) lentils, soaked overnight and drained

150 ml (¼ pint) vegetable stock or water

100 g (4 oz) grated cheese

2 tablespoons chopped fresh herbs

For the sauce

1 onion, finely chopped

1 clove garlic, crushed

1 × 400 g (14 oz) can tomatoes, drained

15 g (½ oz) flour

2 tablespoons tomato ketchup

salt, pepper and tabasco to taste

150 ml (¼ pint) vegetable stock

Preparation time:	15 minutes plus cooling
Cooking time:	18½–21½ minutes
Microwave setting:	High

Cabbage leaves filled with a herby lentil, tomato and cheese stuffing then cooked in a rich tomato sauce

—1—

Put cabbage leaves on to a large plate with 2 tablespoons water. Cover with pierced cling film. Microwave for 1½ minutes. Drain and cool. Remove the hard base of the stalk.

—2—

For the stuffing: Put the oil into a large bowl with the onion and celery. Microwave for 2 minutes. Stir in the tomatoes, lentils and stock. Cover with cling film and microwave for 5 minutes or until the lentils are cooked. Leave to cool while preparing the sauce.

—3—

For the sauce: Put all the ingredients into a jug and mix well. Microwave for 3 minutes or until boiling. Pour into a blender or processor and whizz until sauce is smooth. Taste for seasoning and adjust if necessary.

—4—

Stir the cheese and herbs into the stuffing and add a little seasoning. Divide the stuffing between the leaves and roll up. Put into a greased gratin dish in a single layer and pour over the sauce. Cover and microwave for 7–10 minutes until piping hot.

Stuffed Cabbage and Tomato Bake; Chinese-Style Rice with Egg

Country Vegetable Pie

Serves 6
1 large onion, chopped
1 large carrot, diced
2 tablespoons soya oil
1 × 400 g (14 oz) can tomatoes, drained
1 tablespoon chopped fresh basil or 1 teaspoon dried basil
2 teaspoons tomato purée
100 g (4 oz) mushrooms, sliced
1 × 400 g (14 oz) can canellini beans, drained
225 g (8 oz) courgettes, sliced
1 to 2 tablespoons Worcestershire sauce, or to taste
50 ml (2 fl oz) red wine or vegetable stock
2 bay leaves
salt and pepper
For the topping
1 kg (2 lb) old potatoes, peeled and cubed
25 g (1 oz) butter or margarine
120 ml (4 fl oz) milk
25 g (1 oz) grated Cheddar or vegetarian cheese
1 × 1.75 litre (3 pint) microwave-proof casserole or pie dish

Preparation time:	20 minutes
Cooking time:	35–40 minutes
Microwave setting:	High and conventional grill

—1—

Place the onion and carrot in the casserole, with the oil. Cover the microwave for 6 minutes, stirring halfway through the cooking time.

—2—

Add the drained, chopped tomatoes, basil and tomato purée. Cover and microwave for 2 minutes.

—3—

Stir in the remaining ingredients, cover and microwave for 8–10 minutes until the vegetables are tender. Taste for seasoning and remove the bay leaves.

—4—

Put the potatoes in a large bowl with four tablespoons water. Cover and microwave for 12–14 minutes until they are tender. Drain thoroughly.

—5—

Heat the butter and milk in a small bowl in microwave for 1 minute. Add to the potato and mash until smooth. Spoon or pipe the potato over the vegetables and scatter over the cheese.

—6—

Microwave for 5–6 minutes until heated through. Quickly brown the top under a hot grill and serve immediately.

Spinach and Ricotta Pancakes

Serves 2 to 4
For the pancakes
100 g (4 oz) fine wholemeal flour
a pinch of salt
1 egg, beaten
300 ml (½ pint) milk
15 g (½ oz) butter or margarine, melted
For the filling
225 g (8 oz) frozen chopped spinach, thawed
100 g (4 oz) ricotta cheese
50 g (2 oz) chopped cashews or peanuts
2 egg yolks
2 spring onions, finely chopped
50 ml (2 fl oz) double cream
salt, cayenne and nutmeg to taste
To complete
40 g (1½ oz) butter or margarine
60 g (2 oz) mozzarella, sliced
2 tablespoons grated Parmesan cheese (optional)

Preparation time:	20 minutes
Cooking time:	26–27 minutes
Microwave setting:	High

The wholemeal pancakes are made in the traditional way, then filled with a nutty spinach and ricotta filling

—1—

To make the pancakes: Mix the flour and salt in a bowl. Gradually beat in the egg and the milk to make a smooth batter the consistency of single cream, adding more milk if necessary. Stir in the melted butter.

—2—

Heat a heavy-based frying pan and wipe with an oil-soaked paper towel to lightly grease the entire surface.

—3—

Pour in enough batter to thinly coat the base of the pan. Cook until bubbles appear on the surface, then flip the pancake over and cook until the other side is golden brown. Layer up the cooked pancakes with greaseproof paper and leave to cool. (Pancakes can also be wrapped and frozen when cooled.) The batter should make 8 pancakes.

—4—

For the filling: Squeeze the spinach in a sieve to remove the excess liquid, then put into a bowl and beat in the remaining ingredients. Divide between the pancakes and roll up.

—5—

Arrange in a single layer in a greased gratin dish. Cover with pierced cling film and microwave for 5–7 minutes. Dot with the butter and scatter with the cheese. Microwave for 1½ minutes, and quickly brown under the grill if wished.

Trio of Stuffed Vegetables

Serves 2 to 3

2 medium onions, each about 150 g (5 oz)
2 medium tomatoes
2 large flat mushrooms
40 g (1½ oz) wholemeal breadcrumbs
1 tablespoon chopped fresh parsley
1 tablespoon olive oil
1 clove garlic (or to taste), crushed
40 g (1½ oz) walnut pieces
salt, pepper, tabasco to taste
small knob of butter

Preparation time:	15 minutes
Cooking time:	14–17 minutes
Microwave setting:	High and conventional grill

—1—

Peel the onions and stand upright in a dish. Add two tablespoons water. Cover and microwave for 6–8 minutes, turning over halfway through the cooking time.

—2—

Drain, then scoop out the centres.

—3—

Pierce the skins of the tomatoes with a cocktail stick, then scoop out the centres. Roughly chop onion and tomato centres.

—4—

Remove mushroom stalks and chop roughly. Mix with the breadcrumbs and parsley.

—5—

Put the oil and garlic in a bowl, and microwave for 1 minute. Add to the stuffing with walnuts and seasonings to taste.

—6—

Spoon the filling into the prepared onions, tomatoes and mushrooms. Dot with butter.

—7—

Put the stuffed onions and mushrooms on a flat dish. Cover loosely and microwave for 3 minutes.

—8—

Add the tomatoes to the dish and microwave for a further 3–4 minutes until all the vegetables are tender. Flash under a hot grill before serving.

'Steamed' Date and Nut Pudding

Serves 4

50 g (2 oz) fresh wholemeal breadcrumbs
50 g (2 oz) self-raising wholemeal flour
100 g (4 oz) dates, stoned and roughly chopped
100 g (4 oz) walnuts, roughly chopped
100 g (4 oz) butter or margarine, softened
2 eggs, separated
2 tablespoons milk
1 × 900 ml (1½ pint) pudding basin or
four microwave dariole moulds or teacups

Preparation time:	15 minutes
Cooking time:	5–6 minutes plus standing
Microwave setting:	High

Breadcrumbs make this lovely pudding extra light; dates add sweetness without sugar

—1—

Mix the breadcrumbs with the flour, dates and walnuts.

—2—

Cream butter or margarine until light. Beat in egg yolks one at a time, followed by the milk. Beat until creamy. Fold in the breadcrumb mixture.

—3—

Stiffly whisk the egg whites and carefully fold in. Spoon into the basin or moulds. Cover and microwave for 5–6 minutes.

—4—

Leave to stand for 5 minutes, then turn out and serve immediately, with custard if wished.

'Steamed' Date and Nut Pudding; Apricot Fool; Plum Crumble; Redcurrant Fruit Spread (p 29)

Apricot Fool

Serves 4
175 g (6 oz) ready-to-use dried apricots
300 ml (½ pint) orange juice
1 tablespoon custard powder or cornflour
2 teaspoon sugar (or to taste)
200 ml (7 fl oz) milk
2 tablespoons Amaretto liqueur (optional)
200 ml (7 fl oz) Greek-style yogurt

Preparation time:	10 minutes plus cooling
Cooking time:	12½–15 minutes plus standing
Microwave setting:	High

Dried apricots are an excellent source of vitamins and minerals. They are high in iron and potassium and also contain B vitamins and zinc

—1—

Put the apricots and orange juice into a bowl. Cover and microwave for 10–12 minutes, stirring every 3 minutes.

—2—

Leave to stand for 10 minutes, then drain off all but two tablespoons of the juice (the rest of the juice can be used in fruit salads, etc). Purée the apricots until smooth.

—3—

Mix the custard powder (or cornflour) and sugar with two tablespoons of the milk to make a smooth paste.

—4—

Put the rest of the milk in a jug and microwave for 1½–2 minutes until almost boiling. Stir into the custard powder paste and mix well.

—5—

Return to the microwave and cook for 1 minute, whisking after 30 seconds, to form a smooth, thick custard. Leave to cool.

—6—

Stir in the apricot purée, the liqueur, if using, and swirl in the yogurt to create a "marbled" effect. Pour into glass dishes and serve well-chilled.

Plum Crumble

Serves 4
450 g (1 lb) plums
75–100 g (3–4 oz) demerara sugar, or to taste
For the crumble topping
175 g (6 oz) flour
½ teaspoon mixed spice
100 g (4 oz) butter or margarine
50 g (2 oz) demerara sugar

Preparation time:	10 minutes
Cooking time:	10 minutes
Microwave setting:	High

As an alternative you can substitute rhubarb, or a mixture of apple and blackberry. The crumble freezes well

—1—

Wash, halve and stone the plums. Place in a freezer/microwave-proof dish and toss with the sugar.

—2—

Sieve flour and spice, rub in butter and stir in sugar. Spoon evenly over the fruit.

—3—

To serve immediately: Microwave for 10 minutes.

—4—

To freeze: Cover uncooked crumble with cling film and freeze.

—5—

To serve. Uncover. Microwave on defrost for 10 minutes, stand for 5 minutes, then microwave on high power for 10 minutes. Brown under a hot grill before serving.

● One of the joys of microwave cooking is that the food can be cooked and served in the same dish, which can save on washing up.

● Many china manufacturers have designed elegant freezer-to-microwave-to-table-to dishwasher dinner services, so that you needn't plonk an unattractive kitchen dish on the dinner table amongst your best china.

● To test if a piece of your own china is microwave-proof, pour water into it, then heat in the microwave for 1 minute. The water should be hot, but the sides of the dish should remain cold. Because microwaves act on the water content of food, they don't affect the container. However, dishes will absorb heat from the food.

Potato and Sweetcorn Chowder

Serves 6
1 large onion, sliced
50 g (2 oz) butter or margarine
1 kg (2 lb) potatoes, peeled and cut in chips
450 ml (¾ pint) each boiling milk and water
1 × 350 g (12 oz) can sweetcorn
salt and pepper to taste
1 tablespoon chopped fresh parsley or chives

Preparation time:	10 minutes
Cooking time:	18 minutes
Microwave setting:	High

With wholemeal rolls this soup makes a sustaining and warming meal

Put the onion and butter into a large bowl. Microwave for 2 minutes or until soft. Add the potatoes. Microwave for 1 minute.

—*2*—

Stir the boiling milk and water into the soup with the sweetcorn and a little seasoning. Microwave for 15 minutes.

—*3*—

Taste and adjust the seasoning. Stir in the parsley and serve.

Spicy Lentil Casserole

Serves 4
2 tablespoons soya oil
1 large onion, chopped
2 cloves garlic (or to taste), crushed
2 carrots, peeled and diced
2 sticks celery, diced
225 g (8 oz) red lentils,
washed and soaked for ½ hour
300 ml (½ pint) vegetable stock, boiling hot
450 g (1 lb) tomatoes,
skinned, seeded and chopped
1 tablespoon tomato purée
1 tablespoon each chopped fresh parsley and basil
½ teaspoon each ground cinnamon and paprika
large pinch ground ginger
salt and pepper to taste

Preparation time:	15 minutes plus soaking
Cooking time:	42–45 minutes plus standing
Microwave setting:	High

Lentils and vegetables are cooked with parsley, basil, cinnamon, paprika and ground ginger for a rich, full flavour

Put the oil, onion, garlic, carrots, celery, lentils and stock in a large bowl. Cover and microwave for 12–15 minutes, stirring every 3 minutes. Stir in the remaining ingredients.

—*2*—

Microwave for 30 minutes, stirring every 10 minutes, and adding more stock as necessary.

—*3*—

Leave to stand for 10 minutes. Taste for seasoning, then serve with brown rice.

Variation
To make a thick lentil soup, liquidize the cooked lentil mixture, adding extra vegetable stock to thin down the soup as required.

Baked Avocado Niçoise

Serves 1 as a main dish, 2 as a first course
1 large, ripe avocado
2 tablespoons lemon juice
½ medium tomato, skinned and diced
½ each medium green and red pepper, cored
and finely diced
25 g (1 oz) mozzarella-style cheese, finely diced
1 tablespoon chopped fresh parsley
salt and pepper to taste

Preparation time:	5 minutes
Cooking time:	2½ minutes
Microwave setting:	High

A delicious, pretty supper dish, pretty fast!

—1—

Halve the avocado. Remove the stone but do not peel. Brush the flesh with the lemon juice.

—2—

Mix the remaining ingredients and spoon into hollows in the avocado. Place in individual dishes or a shallow dish. Microwave for 2½ minutes. Serve immediately with crusty bread.

Mango and Lime Sorbet

Serves 8
100 g (4 oz) granulated sugar
2 mangoes
grated rind and juice of 3 limes
2 egg whites, size 3
100 g (4 oz) icing sugar, sifted

Preparation time:	15 minutes plus freezing
Cooking time:	5 minutes
Microwave setting:	High

Choose really ripe, juicy mangoes for this simple sorbet – lovely with fresh fruit salad

—1—

Put the granulated sugar in a bowl with 30 ml (½ pint) water. Microwave for 5 minutes, stirring every minute. Cool.

—2—

Peel the mangoes, and cut the flesh away from the stone. Put the diced flesh into a blender or processor with a little of the sugar syrup and blend until smooth.

—3—

Mix this mango purée into the rest of the syrup and add the grated rind and juice of the limes. Turn into a freezer container and freeze, stirring the mixture every half hour or so until it begins to harden.

—4—

Stiffly whisk the egg whites, and fold in the icing sugar. Fold this meringue mixture in the slushy, semi-frozen purée.

—5—

Return to the freezer. Stir gently after an hour then cover and freeze until firm.

Devilled Potted Shrimps; Turkey Breast Stuffed with Prunes and Almonds; Fluffy Rice; Mangetout; Pear Sorbet in Chocolate Cups (pp 86–87)

The gourmet touch

ENTERTAINING IN STYLE

Trying to prepare an important meal for guests can be nerve-wracking, even for the most experienced cook. The secret is to plan and prepare ahead as much as possible, making good use of both your fridge and freezer, as well as the invaluable microwave. Knowing that you have everything organized gives you the freedom to enjoy a welcoming drink with your guests in peace, instead of rushing frantically round the kitchen, getting all hot and bothered.

Stylish Dinner for Six
Devilled Potted
  Shrimps
Turkey Breast
  Stuffed with
  Prunes and
  Almonds
Fluffy Rice
Mangetout
Pear Sorbet in
  Chocolate Cups

Devilled Potted Shrimps

340 g (12 oz) peeled shrimps
170 g (6 oz) unsalted butter
1 teaspoon ground mace
½ teaspoon mixed spice
½ teaspoon ground pepper
½ teaspoon paprika

Preparation time: 5 minutes
Cooking time: 4 minutes
Microwave setting: Medium, then High

—1—

Pat shrimps dry on kitchen paper. Clarify the butter by microwaving on medium for 2 minutes, then skimming and straining slowly into a clean bowl, discarding the sediment. Put the shrimps into another bowl with enough of the clarified butter to barely moisten. Stir in the spices. Microwave on high for 2 minutes.

—2—

Stir well, then spoon into 6 small ramekin dishes, pressing down firmly. Spoon over the remaining butter to seal and completely cover the shrimps.

—3—

Cool then cover with cling film and chill until firm. Serve garnished with parsley sprigs and lemon wedges.

Turkey Breast Stuffed with Prunes and Almonds

1 boneless turkey breast joint,
  680 to 900 g (1½ to 2 lb)
8 prunes, soaked and stoned
40 g (1½ oz) toasted almonds, chopped
25 g (1 oz) butter or margarine
  salt and pepper to taste
½ teaspoon mild curry powder
4 rashers streaky bacon
140 ml (5 fl oz) double cream (optional)
  watercress to garnish

Preparation time: 15 minutes
Cooking time: 20–25 minutes
Microwave setting: High

—1—

Remove the strings from the breast joint and lay out flat. Arrange the prunes in a line down the centre and sprinkle over the almonds. Season well and dot with half the butter. Roll up again and tie securely with string. Rub the curry powder into the skin, dot with the rest of the butter and wrap in the bacon.

—2—

Place meat, with the join underneath, in an oblong dish. Microwave for 5 minutes, baste, then microwave for a further 10–12 minutes, removing the bacon for the last 5 minutes.

—3—

Remove the strings and carve the joint into thick slices. Place on a warmed serving dish. Stir the cream into the pan juices and microwave for 4–6 minutes, stirring occasionally. Season to taste and serve with the meat, garnished with watercress.

Fluffy Rice

225 g (8 oz) American long grain rice
salt and pepper to taste

Preparation time: 2 minutes
Cooking time: 12–15 minutes
Microwave setting: High

This basic method for cooking rice can be adapted according to your menu – stir in cooked petit pois, toasted nuts, or pine kernels, spices, or fresh herbs

—1—

Put the rice into a large bowl with salt and pepper. Pour over plenty of boiling water.

—2—

Microwave on high for 10–12 minutes, until the rice is tender. Drain. Rinse with cold water and leave to drain thoroughly. Put into a buttered serving dish with plenty of seasoning. When ready to serve, reheat in microwave on high for 2–3 minutes.

Mangetout

455 g (1 lb) mangetout peas, topped and tailed
25 g (1 oz) butter
salt to taste

Preparation time: 15 minutes
Cooking time: 6–7 minutes
Microwave setting: High

—1—

Place the mangetout in a microwave-proof bowl. Sprinkle over one tablespoon water and cover with cling film.

—2—

Microwave on high for 6–7 minutes, shaking the bowl occasionally to turn the mangetout. To serve, sprinkle with salt and dot with butter.

Pear Sorbet in Chocolate Cups

110 g (4 oz) granulated sugar
4 ripe pears, peeled and cored
juice of 1 lemon
few drops of green food colouring (optional)
90 ml (3¼ fl oz) Poire William liqueur
Chocolate cups
85 g (3 oz) good quality white chocolate
10 g (¼ oz) white vegetable fat
mint leaves to garnish

Preparation time: 2 minutes
Cooking time: 12 minutes
Microwave setting: High, then Medium

—1—

Put the sugar in a large bowl with 140 ml (¼ pint) water. Cover with cling film and microwave on high for 5 minutes. Stir, then microwave on high for 2 minutes. Stir. Microwave again on high for 1 minute. Stir and leave to cool.

—2—

Puree the pears in a blender, with the lemon juice. Mix into the cooled sugar syrup with 2 tablespoons of the liqueur and a few drops of food colouring. Pour into a freezer container. Freeze until slushy. Remove from container and beat well. Re-freeze (repeat process if you have the time).

—3—

Meanwhile, make chocolate cups – chop chocolate and put into a small bowl with the fat. Microwave on medium for 1½ to 2 minutes. Stir gently, then use to coat the inside of six paper fairy cake cases (easiest if they're double thickness; use a small spoon to spread the chocolate). Chill until set.

—4—

Place sorbet in freezer container in microwave for 1–2 minutes on high until soft enough to scoop. Meanwhile, remove paper from chocolate cases. Scoop sorbet into chocolate cups. Spoon over the remaining liqueur, garnish and serve immediately.

How to get ahead
● Plan at least one course to be served cold. In warm weather a salad or cold soup makes a refreshing and light start to a meal, but in winter guests will prefer a piping hot soup or spicy, warming first course.
● Be flexible – have a rough idea of what you would like to serve but make the final decision as you shop.

Kipper and Egg Mousse Ring; Medallions of Pork in Sherry Mushroom Sauce; Pommes Dauphinoise; Carrot and Courgette Boulangère

—1—

Mix the mayonnaise with the soured cream. Put the kipper into a shallow buttered dish. Cover with cling film and microwave on high power for 5 minutes. Leave to stand for 2 minutes. Flake fish and leave to cool.

—2—

Put 3 tablespoons water into a cup or small bowl. Sprinkle over the gelatine. Leave until spongy, about 3 minutes. Microwave on low power for 1 minute. Stir – the gelatine should have dissolved. If not, microwave for a few more seconds. Stir into the mousse with the eggs, fish, lemon juice and cayenne to taste. Stiffly whisk the egg white and gently fold in.

—3—

Spoon into the mould and smooth the surface. Cover and chill overnight or until set. Turn out on to a serving plate. Fill the centre of the ring with mustard and cress. Serve with hot toast or melba toast.

Kipper and Egg Mousse Ring

6 eggs, hard-boiled and chopped
150 ml (¼ pint) mayonnaise
150 ml (¼ pint) soured cream
200 g (7 oz) kipper fillet
juice of ½ lemon
cayenne pepper to taste
1 level tablespoon powdered gelatine
1 egg white
mustard and cress to garnish
1 × 900 ml (1½ pint) ring mould, oiled

Preparation time:	15 minutes plus cooling and chilling
Cooking time:	6 minutes plus standing
Microwave setting:	High, then Low

The kipper can be replaced with either smoked haddock, or smoked trout or smoked mackerel, if you wish

Medallions of Pork in Sherry Mushroom Sauce

1 tablespoon oil
750 g (1½ lb) pork fillet
25 g (1 oz) butter or margarine
2 medium onions, thinly sliced
1 tablespoon paprika
2 tablespoons plain flour
4 tablespoons Amontillado sherry
200 ml (7 fl oz) chicken stock
100 g (4 oz) button mushrooms, halved
6 tablespoons single or soured cream
salt and pepper to taste

Preparation time:	15 minutes
Cooking time:	20–25 minutes
Microwave setting:	High

—1—

Heat the oil in a frying pan on top of the stove and quickly fry the pork fillet on both sides. Lift out and drain.

—2—

Meanwhile place the butter, onion and paprika in a microwave-proof casserole. Cover the dish and microwave for 1 minute.

—3—

Stir well then mix in the flour, sherry and stock. Microwave for 1 minute. Stir well then add the pork. Cover and microwave for 15–20 minutes until tender, adding the mushrooms for the final 5 minutes. Take out pork and slice thickly. Place on a warm serving dish.

—4—

Stir the cream into the sauce, taste, then add a little salt and pepper as necessary. Spoon over pork. Garnish with paprika and watercress.

Carrot and Courgette Boulangère

450 g (1 lb) carrots, peeled and sliced
50 g (2 oz) butter or margarine
450 g (1 lb) courgettes, sliced
salt and pepper to taste
1 teaspoon caraway seeds, or to taste
1 microwave-proof gratin dish

Preparation time:	10 minutes
Cooking time:	19½ minutes
Microwave setting:	High, then Medium

—1—

Put the carrots into a bowl of boiling salted water. Microwave for 3 minutes on high power. Rinse with cold water and drain thoroughly.

—2—

Heat the butter or margarine in the gratin dish for 1½ minutes on high power. Add the carrots, courgettes, salt and pepper and caraway seeds. Stir well. Cover and microwave on medium power for 15 minutes, stirring after 7 minutes.

Pommes Dauphinoise

50 g (2 oz) butter or margarine
450 g (1 lb) potatoes, peeled and thinly sliced
1 small onion, thinly sliced
150 ml (¼ pint) single cream
1 egg (size 3), beaten
salt, pepper and grated nutmeg to taste
50 g (2 oz) Gruyère or mild Cheddar cheese, grated
1 microwave-proof gratin dish

Preparation time:	15 minutes
Cooking time:	15 minutes
Microwave setting:	High and conventional grill

A super combination of sliced potatoes, onion, cream and cheese. For a complete supper dish, add more cheese and serve with a crunchy salad

—1—

Melt the butter in the gratin dish in the microwave for 1½ minutes. Using half the potatoes, make a neat layer in the base of the dish. Season well with salt, pepper and nutmeg.

—2—

Cover with the onion slices, then top with the remaining potatoes, neatly arranged. Season again. Cover with cling film and microwave for 9 minutes.

—3—

Remove the dish from the microwave. Whisk the cream with the egg and pour evenly over the potatoes, allowing it to seep down the sides. Cover and microwave for 6 minutes.

—4—

Uncover the dish, sprinkle the cheese over the top and grill until browned. Serve piping hot. (The dish can be browned, then reheated after the pork is cooked. The two vegetable recipes can be cooked together, in a divided dish.)

Winter Dinner for Six
Kipper and Egg Mousse Ring
Medallions of Pork in Sherry Madeira Sauce
Carrot and Courgette Boulangère
Pommes Dauphinoise
Compôte Créole

● Frozen bread rolls can be thawed and warmed in a napkin-lined basket just before serving.
● Slightly under-ripe Brie or Camembert can be ripened on the de-frost setting of your microwave. Cheese biscuits can be crisped up.
● Make a time plan – work out in which order you need to cook/reheat/serve the dishes you plan to serve.

● Choose vegetables that can be cooked ahead then microwaved to serve. Boiled or steamed vegetables can be drained, patted dry with kitchen paper, then layered up in a microwave-proof serving dish with seasoning and a little butter, margarine or sauce, covered and chilled.

● Make soup ahead and chill. Reheat in soup bowls ready to take to the table.

Compôte Creole

100 g (4 oz) granulated sugar
4 large oranges
1 small fresh pineapple
3 bananas
2 tablespoons rum
1 tablespoon toasted flaked almonds

Preparation time:	10 minutes plus cooling and chilling
Cooking time:	8–9 minutes
Microwave setting:	High

Cool and colourful, this caramel-flavoured fruit salad makes an ideal choice to offer after serving a rich main course

—1—

To make the caramel syrup, put the sugar in a bowl with 150 ml (¼ pint) water. Cover with pierced cling film. Microwave for 5 minutes. Stir well, then recover and microwave for 2 minutes. Stir, then microwave uncovered for 1–2 minutes, until mixture turns a light caramel colour. Do not overcook. Stir and leave to cool.

—2—

Using a sharp serrated knife, cut the skin and white pith off the oranges with a spiral sawing movement. Thinly slice the peeled oranges, reserving any juice. Peel and dice the pineapple. Peel and diagonally slice the bananas. Put the fruit in a glass bowl.

—3—

Pour over the rum, caramel syrup and any reserved orange juice. Chill until ready to serve, then sprinkle with the browned almond flakes.

Spiced Watercress Soup

50 g (2 oz) butter or margarine
1 large onion, finely chopped
1½ teaspoons ground coriander
2 tablespoons plain flour
1.2 litres (2 pints) chicken stock
2 bunches fresh watercress
salt and pepper to taste
150 ml (¼ pint) single cream

Preparation time:	10 minutes
Cooking time:	14 minutes
Microwave setting:	High and Medium

—1—

Put the butter or margarine in a bowl. Microwave on high power until melted.

—2—

Stir in the onion. Cover with cling film. Microwave on medium power for 2 minutes. Stir in the coriander. Recover and microwave on high power for 30 seconds.

—3—

Stir in the flour, then the stock. Microwave on high power for 5 minutes. Stir well, then microwave on high for 5 minutes.

—4—

Reserve some watercress for garnish; put the remainder in the soup and blend until smooth. Season and add cream. Pour into soup bowls and reheat.

Tomato and Pepper Salad

450 g (1 lb) tomatoes, skinned
2 peppers, cored and seeded
2 tablespoons wine vinegar
4 tablespoons olive oil
salt and pepper to taste
1 teaspoon chive-flavoured mustard
½ teaspoon caster sugar

Preparation time: 10 minutes

—*1*—

Thinly slice the tomatoes and peppers. Neatly arrange in layers in a glass serving bowl.

—*2*—

Put all the dressing ingredients in a screw-topped jar and shake well until emulsified. Pour over the salad.

Dilled Potato Salad

450 g (1 lb) small new potatoes, scrubbed
3–4 sprigs dill
sea salt, and pepper
For the dressing
3 tablespoons olive oil
1 tablespoon wine vinegar
1 tablespoon chive-flavoured mustard
2 shallots or spring onions, finely chopped
4 anchovy fillets, drained and chopped
1 tablespoon chopped dill

Preparation time:	10 minutes
Cooking time:	15–18 minutes
Microwave setting:	High

—*1*—

Put the potatoes into a large bowl with the dill and a little sea salt and pepper. Pour over enough boiling water to cover. Cover with pierced cling film and microwave for 15–18 minutes until the potatoes are tender. (Reduce the setting to 'medium' if the water boils too vigorously.)

—*2*—

Meanwhile, put all the dressing ingredients in a screw-topped jar and shake until emulsified.

—*3*—

Drain the cooked potatoes, and put into a warmed serving bowl. Pour over the dressing and toss gently but thoroughly. Garnish with chopped dill.

Baked Trout with Ham Stuffing

1 fresh farmed pink or sea trout (about 1.5 kg 3 lb)
25 g (1 oz) butter or margarine
1 large microwave Roast-in-Bag
For the stuffing
2 × 175 g (6 oz) smoked trout, boned
50 g (2 oz) cooked ham, finely diced
50 g (2 oz) fresh white breadcrumbs
2 tablespoons finely chopped parsley
juice of ½ lemon
3 teaspoons creamed horseradish
2 egg yolks
1 tablespoon single cream or top of the milk
To garnish
thin slices of lemon, parsley sprigs

Preparation time:	25 minutes
Cooking time:	8–10 minutes
Microwave setting:	High

—*1*—

Spread the butter or margarine inside a large microwave Roast-in-Bag.

—*2*—

Put the smoked trout into a bowl with the ham, breadcrumbs and chopped parsley. Mix well. Beat the lemon juice, creamed horseradish and egg yolk together. Add to the stuffing with the cream. Fill the inside of the trout with the stuffing, reforming it into a neat shape.

—*3*—

Place the fish in the bag, securing it with an elastic band. Place on microwave turntable or on a large plate. Microwave for 8–10 minutes, turning the fish over halfway through the cooking time.

—*4*—

Remove fish from microwave, snip off elastic band and slit the bag open. Using a small knife, skin the top of the fish, removing the fin. Lifting it on the Roast-in-Bag, roll the fish over on to a hot serving plate, skinned side downwards. Carefully lift off the remaining skin. Garnish with lemon and parsley and serve with mayonnaise.

Midsummer Dinner for Six
Spiced
   Watercress
   Soup
Tomato and
   Pepper Salad
Baked Trout with
   Ham Stuffing
Dilled Potato
   Salad
Grand Marnier
   Crème Caramel

Grand Marnier Crème Caramel

For the custard

4 eggs

50 g (2 oz) caster sugar

½ teaspoon vanilla essence

600 ml (1 pint) milk

50 ml (2 fl oz) Grand Marnier

For the caramel

35 g (1¼ oz) granulated sugar

1 tablespoon water

90 ml (3¼ fl oz) Grand Marnier

1 × 1 litre (1¾ pint) straight-sided soufflé dish

Preparation time:	10 minutes
Cooking time:	12–16 minutes
Microwave setting:	High, then Low

Spiced Watercress Soup (p 90); Baked Trout with Ham Stuffing (p 91); Dilled Potato Salad (p 91); Tomato and Pepper Salad (p 90); Grand Marnier Crème Caramel

—1—

Beat together all the custard ingredients.

—2—

Put sugar and water for the caramel into the soufflé dish and microwave on high power until it is a good caramel colour, about 3–5 minutes. Using an oven cloth, take the dish out of the cooker and tip the caramel round it to coat the base and sides evenly. Let it cool for a few minutes until set.

—3—

Strain the custard mixture on to the caramel and cover the dish with cling film. Microwave on high power for 1 minute, then on low power for 8–10 minutes.

—4—

Remove the cling film and allow to cool. When cold turn on to a plate and pour over the Grand Marnier.

Summertime Salmon Trout

Serves 4 to 6
1 × 1¼–1½ kg (2½–3 lb) salmon trout
100 g (4 oz) sorrel leaves, cleaned
For the stuffing
1 shallot finely chopped
50 g (2 oz) mushrooms, trimmed and finely
chopped
½ medium cucumber, peeled
50 g (2 oz) granary breadcrumbs
1 tablespoon lemon juice
1 tablespoon chopped fresh dill
1 egg, beaten
salt and pepper to taste
25 g (1 oz) butter

Preparation time:	25 minutes
Cooking time:	12–18 minutes
Microwave setting:	High

—1—

Trim the tail of the fish and cut off the fins. Pat dry on paper towels.

—2—

Blanch the sorrel in boiling salted water for 1 minute then drain and rinse with cold water. Drain well.

—3—

For the stuffing: Halve the cucumber lengthways and scoop out the seeds, using a teaspoon. Finely chop the cucumber flesh and mix with the shallot, mushrooms and breadcrumbs, lemon juice and dill. Stir in the egg and season well.

—4—

Carefully spoon the stuffing into the cavity of the fish. Wrap the sorrel leaves (like a bandage) around the fish, then dot with the butter, and sprinkle lightly with pepper. Wrap the fish in oiled greaseproof paper, then microwave on high power for 12–18 minutes or until the flesh flakes easily.

—5—

Unwrap, and serve with home-made mayonnaise flavoured with dill.

Crunchy Cauliflower Salad

1 large cauliflower
1 × 300 g (11 oz) tin sweetcorn, drained
1 head celery, washed and shredded
50 g (2 oz) walnut pieces, chopped
2 or 3 red apples
juice of ½ large lemon
2 tablespoons snipped chives
2 tablespoons chopped parsley
300 ml (½ pint) French dressing

Preparation time:	10 minutes plus chilling
Cooking time:	2 minutes
Microwave setting:	High

—1—

Cut the cauliflower into florets. Rinse well. Place in a large bowl with 2 tablespoons water and a pinch of salt. Cover with pierced cling film and microwave for 2 minutes. Leave to cool, carefully drain off any liquid.

—2—

Stir in the sweetcorn, celery and walnuts. Quarter and core the apples, leaving them unpeeled. Chop roughly, toss in the lemon juice and add to the salad.

—3—

Add the herbs to the dressing and pour over, tossing well. Arrange in a large salad bowl and chill until ready to serve.

Summer Buffet Party For 15
Summertime
 Salmon Trout
Crunchy
 Cauliflower
 Salad
Pressed Turkey
 Terrine
Sole and Smoked
 Salmon
 Roulades
Pepper, Tomato
 and Courgette
 Salad
Spinach Potato
 Salad
Rich Orange
 Mousse
Fresh Raspberry
 Tart

● Cooking times will vary according to the starting temperature of the food – food cooked from room temperature will take less time than that which is taken from the fridge or freezer.
● Take care when heating fruit pies or pastries with a sweet filling (such as mince pies) as the filling can easily burn before the pastry feels warm. A mince pie can be sufficiently heated in 10 seconds. Stand bread and pastry on kitchen paper to prevent sogginess.
● Stale coffee beans can regain their fresh aroma and flavour in the microwave.

Pressed Turkey Terrine

1 kg (2 lb) turkey breast meat, thinly sliced
finely grated rind of 1 lemon
4 tablespoons lemon juice
3 tablespoons chopped parsley
½ teaspoon chopped fresh thyme
1 tablespoon snipped fresh chives
For the mousse
1 kg (2 lb) turkey leg meat
150 ml (¼ pint) double cream
1 egg, size 3
1 teaspoon salt
freshly ground black pepper
225 g (8 oz) smoked streaky bacon
1 × 1.75 litre (3 pint) oblong microwave-proof
loaf pan or terrine
To garnish
lemon slices, fresh parsley, or dill sprigs

Preparation time:	30 minutes plus cooling
Cooking time:	1 hour 5 minutes
Microwave setting:	Medium

—1—

Put the turkey into a bowl with the lemon rind and juice and leave to marinade.

—2—

Skin the leg meat, cut into small pieces and remove all sinews and tendons. Mince finely or process in the food processor. Add the cream, egg, salt and pepper, and beat until smooth.

—3—

Remove the rind from the bacon, carefully stretch each slice with the back of a heavy-bladed knife and cut in half. Line the base of the loaf pan with about a third of the marinaded breast slices. Cover with half the streaky bacon and half the herbs. Then spread half the mousse mixture on top. Repeat with another layer of marinaded breast meat and layer up as before, finishing with a final layer of turkey breasts. Pour over any lemon juice left in the bowl.

—4—

Cover tightly with cling film and place in a baking dish half-filled with warm water and microwave for 1 hour 5 minutes. Test the meat with a sharp knife or skewer; it should be tender and the juices should run clear.

—5—

Remove from the baking dish. Press with a 1 kg (2 lb) weighted saucer and leave to cool. Drain off most of the juices from meat. The turkey terrine can be wrapped and chilled for up to 3 days or frozen for up to 3 months.

Sole and Smoked Salmon Roulades

10 medium fillets of sole (or plaice), skinned
350 g (12 oz) sliced smoked salmon
juice of 1 lemon
Rice salad
450 g (1 lb) American long grain rice
450 g (1 lb) button mushrooms
a squeeze of lemon
450 g (1 lb) frozen peas 'petit pois'
450 g (1 lb) shelled prawns
salt and pepper to taste
150 ml (¼ pint) French dressing
Curried mayonnaise
1 small onion, thinly sliced
2 tablespoons oil
2 cloves garlic, crushed
1 tablespoon mild curry powder
300 ml (½ pint) tinned tomato juice
salt and pepper to taste
half a lemon
2 tablespoons mango chutney (or apricot jam)
300 ml (½ pint) mayonnaise
a bunch of watercress to garnish

Preparation time:	35 minutes plus cooling and chilling
Cooking time:	26–28 minutes
Microwave setting:	Medium, then High

—1—

Cut each sole in half to give 20 long single fillets. Cut the smoked salmon in strips wide enough to cover each fillet of sole. Roll up neatly and stand the roulades upright in a buttered microwave-proof baking dish. Make up the lemon juice to half a pint with water; pour over the fish, add a sprinkling of salt and cover with pierced cling film. Cook in the microwave on medium power for 6 minutes or until the fish turns white. Remove and allow to cool in the liquid. Drain and cover, then chill or freeze.

—2—

Cook the rice in the microwave as for Fluffy Rice (page 87), then drain and run under hot water to loosen the grains. Drain and then cool.

—3—

Trim the mushrooms and quarter. Put into a dish with a squeeze of lemon juice. Cover with cling film and microwave on high power for 45 seconds. Drain and leave to cool. Tip the frozen peas into a dish. Cover with cling film and microwave on high power for 9–11 minutes, stirring twice during that time, until tender. Leave to cool.

—4—

Stir the peas, mushrooms and prawns into the rice with a little seasoning.

—5—

Put the sliced onion and oil into a bowl. Mix well then cover with cling film. Microwave on medium power for 2 minutes. Stir in the crushed garlic and curry powder. Cover and microwave for 3½ minutes on high power. Stir in the tomato juice and a very little salt and pepper, half a lemon (left intact) and the chutney. Microwave on high power for 5 minutes uncovered. Strain and make up to 250 ml (8 fl oz) with tomato juice. Leave to cool completely.

—6—

Mix the curry sauce into the mayonnaise, whisking until smooth. If necessary, add a drop of boiling water to make a thin coating consistency and taste for seasoning.

To get ahead:
● The day before – Make the Turkey Terrine, wrap and chill (can also be frozen for up to 3 months). Make the Sole and Smoked Salmon Roulades and Rice Salad. Wrap and chill (can also be frozen for up to 1 month). Make the Potato Salad, wrap and chill.
● Make the Mayonnaise the day before. Make the Orange Mousse (can also be frozen).
● Two hours before the party, finish all the recipes and transfer to serving bowls.

—7—

To serve: Put the rice salad on to a serving dish and arrange the sole roulades on top. Spoon a tablespoon of the curried mayonnaise over each roll and garnish with watercress. Serve the rest of the curried mayonnaise in a separate bowl.

Pepper, Tomato and Courgette Salad

2 large red peppers
2 large green peppers
450 g (1 lb) young courgettes
1 small onion, finely chopped
4 large tomatoes
50 g (2 oz) stuffed green olives
300 ml (½ pint) French dressing

Preparation time: 10 minutes

—1—

Halve the peppers, remove the core and seeds, wash and dry. Shred finely with a sharp knife. Top and tail the courgettes, rinse and dry. Slice thinly in diagonal slices. Chop the onion as finely as possible. Wash and dry the tomatoes and cut into eighths. Halve the stuffed olives.

—2—

Toss all the vegetables together in the French dressing and arrange in a serving dish.

Pepper, Tomato and Courgette Salad (p 95); Spinach Potato Salad; Fresh Raspberry Tart; Rich Orange Mousses; Sole and Smoked Salmon Roulades with Rice Salad (p 94); Pressed Turkey Terrine (p 94); Crunchy Cauliflower Salad (p 93); Celebration Punch (p 101)

Spinach Potato Salad

2¼ kg (5 lb) small new potatoes, scrubbed
225 g (8 oz) frozen chopped spinach
600 ml (1 pint) mayonnaise
150 ml (¼ pint) single cream
1 clove garlic, crushed (or to taste)
salt and pepper to taste
¼ teaspoon grated nutmeg

Preparation time:	15 minutes plus cooling and chilling
Cooking time:	24–27 minutes plus standing
Microwave setting:	High

—1—

Put half the potatoes into a large bowl with a little salt. Pour over enough boiling water to cover, then cover with pierced cling film and microwave for 15–18 minutes, depending on size, until tender and cooked through. Drain and cool. Cook remaining potatoes in the same way and set aside.

—2—

Put the frozen spinach into a dish. Microwave for 9 minutes, or according to instructions on packet, stirring after 4 minutes. Stand for 2 minutes, then drain well and press in a fine sieve to remove as much liquid as possible, then cool.

—3—

Mix the mayonnaise, cream, spinach and seasonings together. Taste and adjust accordingly. Carefully mix two-thirds of the green mayonnaise with the potatoes. Cover with cling film and chill overnight to let the flavours penetrate the potatoes.

—4—

Next day, put the potatoes in a serving dish and spoon over the remaining spinach mayonnaise mixture.

Rich Orange Mousse

1 × 175 ml (6 fl oz) plastic container frozen
concentrated orange juice
6 eggs, separated
175 g (6 oz) caster sugar
grated rind of 2 oranges
450 ml (¾ pint) double or whipping cream
2 sachets gelatine
juice of 2 lemons, made up to 150 ml (¼ pint)
with orange juice
150 ml (¼ pint) double or whipping cream
chocolate to decorate
a piping bag and star pipe

Preparation time:	20 minutes plus chilling
Cooking time:	3 minutes
Microwave setting:	Low

—1—

Put plastic container of orange juice into
the microwave, and defrost on low power
for 2 minutes. Put the juice into a mixer
bowl with the egg yolks, orange rind and
sugar and beat together until thick enough
to leave a trail across the surface.

—2—

Whip the cream until soft but holding its
shape. Sprinkle the gelatine over the lemon
and orange juice in a small bowl. Leave
until absorbed. Dissolve in the microwave
for 1 minute. Stir gently. Add to the mousse
with the whipped cream. Whip the egg
whites until stiff and fold in carefully. Pour
into the serving bowl or bowls, cover and
refrigerate.

—3—

To complete, whip the remaining cream
until stiff. Fill a piping bag with a star pipe
attached and pipe stars around the edge.
Chill until ready to serve. Decorate with
chocolate thins, squares or just grated
chocolate. Serve at room temperature.

Fresh Raspberry Tart

150 g (5 oz) digestive biscuits, crushed
25 g (1 oz) caster sugar
pinch cinnamon
50 g (2 oz) butter or margarine
225 g (8 oz) Philadelphia cream cheese
grated rind and juice of 1 orange
25 g (1 oz) caster sugar
3 tablespoons double cream
225 g (8 oz) raspberries
2 tablespoons redcurrant jelly
1 × 20 cm (8 in) flan dish

Preparation time:	15 minutes plus chilling
Cooking time:	4–5 minutes
Microwave setting:	High

—1—

Mix the biscuits with the sugar and cinnamon. Put the butter in a separate bowl.
Melt it in the microwave for 2 minutes. Mix
into the biscuits and press on to the base
and sides of the flan dish.

—2—

Put the cream cheese into a bowl. Microwave for 1 minute. Remove, and beat in the
orange rind and juice, sugar and cream.
Spoon into the flan dish and smooth the
surface.

—3—

Chill until set, then cover with the raspberries. Melt the jelly in the microwave for 1–2
minutes, and gently brush over the top of
the raspberries to glaze. Chill and serve.

● Using a microwave is by far the best way to cook vegetables. The results are equally impressive with both simple vegetable dishes and our slightly more adventurous recipes. This is because microwaved vegetables retain their shape, colour, flavour and texture more readily than with conventional cooking. Fruit and pulses also microwave effectively and, as all are cooked with the minimum amount of liquid, fewer precious vitamins are lost.

Potage Vert

Serves 6 to 8

1 medium onion, finely chopped
25 g (1 oz) butter
225 g (8 oz) potato, peeled and cubed
225 g (8 oz) courgettes, topped, tailed and chopped
1 small bunch watercress, stalks removed
225 g (8 oz) shelled fresh peas
100 g (4 oz) fresh spinach, washed and stalks removed
1 litre (1¾ pints) good quality chicken stock
1 bay leaf
salt, pepper and cayenne, all to taste
150 ml (¼ pint) single cream
To garnish
a little chopped fresh chives and mint

Preparation time:	20 minutes plus cooling and chilling
Cooking time:	19–22 minutes
Microwave setting:	High

A chilled, green summer soup that's full of taste and goodness, as well as being a very simple dish to prepare

—1—

Put the onion in a large bowl with the butter and potato. Cover and microwave for 6 minutes.

—2—

Add the remaining vegetables. Cover and microwave for 6–8 minutes or until potato is tender.

—3—

Add the stock and bay leaf and stir well. Microwave for 7–8 minutes. Remove bay leaf.

—4—

Process or liquidize the soup until smooth. Stir in cream and season to taste. Cool then chill and serve in chilled soup bowls garnished with chopped chives and mint.

Mortadelle d'Agneau

Serves 6 to 8

1 large boned shoulder of lamb (prepared weight about 1½ kg/3 lb)
1 × ¼ in slice cooked ham
25 g (1 oz) mushrooms, chopped
1 clove garlic, crushed
12 green peppercorns (the bottled or canned variety), optional
4 tablespoons chopped fresh parsley
1 egg, beaten
1 tablespoon oil
150 ml (¼ pint) mixture of white wine and stock
a bouquet garni
a sprig of rosemary
salt and pepper to taste

Preparation time:	20 minutes plus chilling overnight
Cooking time:	45 minutes plus standing
Microwave setting:	High, then Medium and conventional hob

Ask the butcher to remove the bones from a 1¾ kg (4 lb) shoulder of lamb. The lamb is then stuffed with a quickly-prepared mixture of ham and mushrooms, cooked, and served hot or cold

—1—

Trim off as much fat as possible from the lamb. Then trim a small piece of lean meat from the thickest part of the shoulder and cut into finger-like strips. Cut the ham into similar strips also.

—2—

Put the mushrooms and garlic into a bowl with the peppercorns, parsley and egg. Season lightly.

—3—

Lay the lamb, with skin side facing down, on a work surface. Lightly season the meat, then arrange the strips of ham and lamb and the mushroom filling evenly on top. Roll up and tie securely with fine string. Quickly brown the meat in the oil, in a heavy pan on top of the stove.

● To test whether or not a container is microwave-proof, fill it a third full with cold water. Microwave on high for 2 minutes. If the container remains cool and the water is warm, then it is suitable for use.

—4—

Transfer to a large microwave-proof dish and pour over the wine and stock. Add the bouquet garni, rosemary and a little seasoning.

—5—

Cover and microwave on high power for 6 minutes, then on medium power for 35 minutes. Leave to stand for 5 minutes, covered with a tent of foil. The lamb should be cooked and tender. Leave to cool, then chill overnight. Serve thinly sliced with the Broad Bean Salad (see recipe) and a potato salad.

Variation
This recipe can also be served hot.

Broad Bean Salad

Serves 6 to 8
750 g (1½ lb) shelled young broad beans
1 tablespoon chopped fresh mint
3 tablespoons olive oil
1 tablespoon white wine vinegar
salt and pepper to taste

Preparation time:	10 minutes
Cooking time:	6–8 minutes
Microwave setting:	High

Broad beans are as good cold in a salad as they are hot. To turn this salad into a main dish, add some diced ham or cooked chicken, cut into strips

—1—

Put the beans in a large bowl with four tablespoons water. Cover and microwave for 6–8 minutes until tender. Drain and cool slightly. If you have the time, remove the tough, greyish outer skin from the beans.

—2—

Put all the remaining ingredients in a screw-topped jar and shake until emulsified.

—3—

Toss the warm beans in the dressing and taste for seasoning. Serve warm, or leave until cold and serve chilled.

'Green' Rice Salad

Serves 6
225 g (8 oz) long grain rice, washed
6 spring onions, finely sliced
50 g (2 oz) toasted pine nuts or cashew nuts
50 g (2 oz) pumpkin seeds
1 green pepper, cored and thinly sliced
For the dressing
6 tablespoons olive oil
2 tablespoons white wine vinegar
salt and pepper to taste
2 tablespoons chopped fresh herbs

Preparation time:	10 minutes
Cooking time:	10–12 minutes
Microwave setting:	High

Delicious with cold roast chicken, this salad is full of 'green' ingredients – spring onions for flavour, pumpkin seeds for goodness and crunch, green pepper to add a tang, and a herby dressing too

—1—

Put the rice into a large bowl. Pour over plenty of boiling water to cover well. Microwave for 10–12 minutes until rice is tender, but do not overcook. Drain and rinse with cold water. Drain thoroughly.

—2—

Mix the cold rice with the spring onions, pine or cashew nuts, pumpkin seeds and green pepper.

—3—

Put all the ingredients for the dressing in a screw-topped jar and shake until emulsified. Pour over the rice and mix well before serving.

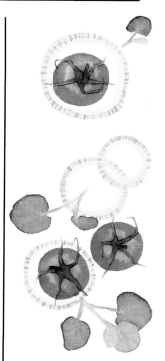

Potage Vert (p 98); Mortadella d'Agneau with Broad Bean Salad (p 98–99); 'Green' Rice Salad (p 99); Cold Blackcurrant Soufflé with Cassis Sauce

Cold Blackcurrant Soufflé

Serves 4 to 6

For the soufflé

350 g (12 oz) fresh or frozen blackcurrants

50 ml (2 fl oz) cassis

4 eggs, separated

150 g (5 oz) caster sugar

1 tablespoon powdered gelatine

210 ml (7½ fl oz) whipping or double cream, lightly whipped

extra whipped cream and a few sprigs of mint leaves for decorating

For the sauce

6 tablespoons blackcurrant jelly or jam

3 tablespoons cassis

1 tablespoon lemon juice

1 × 1.75 litre (3 pint) glass bowl or soufflé case

Preparation time:	25 minutes plus soaking and chilling
Cooking time:	13 minutes
Microwave setting:	Defrost, then High

—1—

Put the blackcurrants into a large bowl and place in the microwave (if using frozen fruit, microwave on defrost for 8 minutes until thawed, before continuing with the recipe). Microwave on high power for 3 minutes until the fruit is very soft.

—2—

Purée the fruit in a blender or processor, then sieve to remove the pips. Stir in the cassis and leave to cool.

—3—

Add the egg yolks and sugar to the blackcurrant purée and beat well. Microwave on high power for 30 seconds then whisk until very thick and pale. (This is easily done using an electric mixer.) The mixture should form a ribbon-like trail when the whisk is lifted.

—4—

Put two tablespoons water in a small bowl and sprinkle over the gelatine. Leave to soak for 5 minutes then microwave on high power for 15–30 seconds until dissolved. Stir into the blackcurrant mixture.

—5—

Fold in the lightly-whipped cream, then whisk the egg whites until stiff and carefully fold in, in two batches.

—6—

Spoon into the dish and chill until set. Decorate with rosettes of whipped cream and sprigs of mint leaves. Chill until ready to serve.

—7—

For the sauce: Put the jam into a bowl (not plastic) and microwave on high power for 1 minute. Sieve to make a smooth, runny sauce then stir in the cassis and lemon juice. Reheat if necessary. Serve the sauce hot or cool with the chilled soufflé.

Celebration Punch

2 × 1 litre (1¾ pint) cartons fresh orange juice
6 × 750 ml (1¼ pint) bottles sparkling pomagne dry cider, chilled
half a large bottle of white rum
a lime or small lemon or orange

Preparation time: 5 minutes

—1—

Put a tablespoon of lime into each glass and add two or three tablespoons fresh orange juice to each.

—2—

Top up with chilled pomagne and garnish with small pieces of sliced fruit.

Variation
Mix all ingredients together in a punch bowl or several large glass jugs.

Date Flapjacks

175 g (6 oz) finely chopped dates
2 teaspoons runny honey
100 g (4 oz) butter or margarine
100 g (4 oz) plain flour
75 g (3 oz) soft light brown sugar
120 g (4½ oz) rolled oats
1 × 20 cm (8 in) shallow round baking dish, greased

Preparation time: 15 minutes
Cooking time: 16½ minutes
Microwave setting: High and Medium

Inexpensive chopped dates for baking are readily available from supermarkets

—1—

Put the dates, honey and 85 ml (3 fl oz) water into a medium-sized bowl and stir until mixed. Microwave on high power for 4 minutes. Cover with cling film and leave to stand.

—2—

In another bowl, rub the fat into the flour, until the mixture resembles fine crumbs. Stir in the sugar and oats.

—3—

Press two-thirds of the mixture into a deep (20 cm/8 in) shallow round dish or a similar sized square container. Microwave on medium power for 5 minutes. Spoon the date mixture evenly over the oats and sprinkle with remaining oat mixture. Press down lightly. Microwave on high power for 7½ minutes. Mark into 10 wedges or fingers while still warm and leave to cool in the container.

—4—

When cold, turn out and cool on a wire rack. Serve cut into wedges or fingers. A popular 'any time' munch.

Afternoon Tea For 10
Date Flapjacks
Chocolate Orange Layer Cake
Banana and Apple Teabread
Dundee Cake
Jubilee Biscuit Cake

Chocolate Orange Layer Cake

150 ml (¼ pint) soya oil
100 g (4 oz) plain flour
25 g (1 oz) cocoa powder
2 teaspoons baking powder
25 g (1 oz) cornflour
100 g (4 oz) caster sugar
2 egg whites
For the filling
200 ml (7 fl oz) double cream, whipped
3 oranges, peeled and segmented
for the topping
100 g (4 oz) plain chocolate, broken up
1 × 20 cm (8 in) deep soufflé case or microwave
ware cake pan, base-lined

Preparation time:	20 minutes
Cooking time:	6½–8 minutes
Microwave setting:	High, then Medium

This is a light, fluffy sponge cake filled with whipped cream

—1—

Blend the oil with an equal quantity of cold water. Sift the flour with the cocoa powder, baking powder and cornflour into a mixing bowl. Gradually beat in the oil mixture, followed by the sugar, to form a smooth batter.

—2—

Stiffly whisk the egg whites and fold in. Spoon into the prepared dish. Microwave on high power for 5–6 minutes. Leave to stand for 10 minutes, then turn out on to a wire rack and leave to cool.

—3—

Cut the cold cake horizontally into three layers. Sandwich with the cream and orange segments.

—4—

Put the chocolate in a small bowl and microwave on medium for 1½–2 minutes until spreadable. Using a round bladed knife, swirl the chocolate on top of the cake and leave to set.

Banana and Apple Teabread

Makes 2 small loaves
225 g (8 oz) very ripe bananas, peeled
100 g (4 oz) eating apples, weighed after peeling
and coring
a few drops of lemon juice
50 g (2 oz) butter or margarine
100 g (4 oz) soft dark brown sugar
150 ml (¼ pint) milk or milk and water mixed
1 egg, beaten
100 g (4 oz) plain flour
100 g (4 oz) wholemeal flour
1 teaspoon bicarbonate of soda
2 × 900 ml (1½ pints) microwave-proof loaf pans

Preparation time:	15 minutes plus cooling
Cooking time:	13½–16½ minutes plus standing
Microwave setting:	High

Treat yourself to afternoon tea in the garden and enjoy this moist teabread spread with butter and honey

—1—

Mash the bananas, then finely chop the apples. Mix together and sprinkle with lemon juice to prevent the fruits from turning brown.

—2—

Place the butter, sugar and milk in a jug. Microwave for 1½ minutes, or until the butter has melted. Mix in the egg.

—3—

Mix the flours with the bicarbonate of soda, then stir in the melted mixture and the prepared fruits. Beat until well mixed.

—4—

Spoon into the loaf pans and smooth the surface. Microwave for 12–15 minutes until firm. Leave to stand for 5 minutes, then turn out and leave to cool.

—5—

Serve warm or at room temperature, buttered. The teabread freezes well for up to 6 weeks.

Dundee Cake

175 g (6 oz) butter or margarine, softened
175 g (6 oz) soft dark brown sugar
3 eggs, beaten
2 tablespoons black treacle
2 tablespoons brandy
100 g (4 oz) plain flour
100 g (4 oz) self-raising flour
2 tablespoons mixed spice
a pinch of salt
750 g (1½ lb) mixed dried fruit (sultanas, raisins, etc)
50 g (2 oz) chopped nuts
50 g (2 oz) glacé cherries, chopped
For decoration
40 g (1½ oz) split blanched almonds
50 g (2 oz) glacé cherries, halved
1 × 19 cm (7½ in) straight-sided, deep container, lined and greased

Preparation time:	15 minutes plus cooling
Cooking time:	44 minutes plus standing
Microwave setting:	Defrost

Any straight-sided, non-metallic container, such as a soufflé case, can be used for baking cakes in a microwave

—1—

Beat the butter or margarine with the sugar until light and fluffy. Gradually beat in the eggs, treacle and brandy.

—2—

Sieve together the flours, spice and salt. Carefully fold into the creamed mixture, followed by the fruit, nuts and cherries. Spoon into the prepared container. Cook in the microwave for 20 minutes.

—3—

Arrange the split almonds and cherries on

● To thaw frozen puff pastry, microwave on high for 1 minute, turning over after 30 seconds. Stand for 6 minutes before rolling
● If you want to make a ring-shaped caked but don't have a ring mould, use a straight-sided round dish with a straight-sided jar in the centre.

the top of the cake in a neat pattern. Cook for a further 24 minutes, then leave to stand for 5 minutes before turning out. Cool on a wire rack. This cake will keep well in an airtight container and can also be frozen.

Jubilee Biscuit Cake

100 g (4 oz) unsalted butter
1 tablespoon caster sugar
1 tablespoon golden syrup
2 teaspoons cocoa powder
50 g (2 oz) sultanas
25 g (1 oz) glacé cherries, roughly chopped
225 g (8 oz) digestive biscuits, crushed
90 g (3½ oz) plain chocolate
1 × 18 cm (7 in) square container or tin

Preparation time:	15 minutes, plus setting
Cooking time:	4 minutes
Microwave setting:	High, then Medium

A really quick recipe that tastes heavenly – it's full of cherries, sultanas and chocolate

—1—

Put the butter and sugar into a large bowl. Microwave on high power for 1½ minutes. Stir in the syrup, cocoa, sultanas and cherries. Microwave on high power for 30 seconds. Mix in the digestive crumbs and spoon into the container or tin and smooth the surface. Leave to set.

—2—

Put the broken up chocolate into a bowl. Microwave on medium power for 2 minutes or until smooth and spreadable. Using a round-bladed knife, spread the chocolate over the biscuit base. Leave until set, then cut into squares or fingers.

*Marseillaise Beef
Casserole (p 107)*

A taste of the great cuisines

INTERNATIONAL FLAVOURS

Using your microwave creatively, it is possible to capture a variety of flavours and cooking styles from around the world. Try out the increasingly popular Indian cuisine, or be more adventurous and sample Chinese – the microwave is perfect for cooking fish and vegetables the Chinese way, sealing in the flavour and freshness. Mexican food has an intriguing combination of creamy and crunchy textures, while the more familiar dishes of France and Italy will bring back happy memories of sun-filled holidays and delicious meals.

French Menu
Tapénade
Marseillaise Beef
 Casserole
 or
Avignon Lamb
 with Beans
 or
Lapin Moutarde
French Beans
 with Ham
Chocolate Mocha
 Pots

Tapénade

Serves 6

75 g (3 oz) black olives, stoned
1 clove garlic, crushed
6 anchovy fillets
2 tablespoons capers
juice of 1 lemon
freshly ground black pepper to taste
2 tablespoons chopped fresh basil
4–6 tablespoons olive oil
1 large or 2 small baguettes/French sticks

Preparation time:	10 minutes
Cooking time:	2–3 minutes
Microwave setting:	High

A well-flavoured black olive pâté to eat (as here) with a baguette, crispy French bread, or alternatively serve tossed with hot pasta

—1—

Put all the ingredients, except the oil, basil and French bread, in a processor or blender. Process until the mixture forms a thick, rough paste. Stir in the basil, then beat in the oil a drop at a time to make a spreadable paste.

—2—

Thinly slice the bread as if making garlic bread (that is, not completely through to the base of the bread). Spread the slices with the paste, then wrap the stick or sticks in greaseproof paper.

—3—

Microwave for 2–3 minutes, until heated through. Serve hot.

Avignon Lamb with Beans

Serves 6

1 kg (2 lb) boned shoulder or leg of lamb, trimmed and cubed
175 g (6 oz) carrots, sliced
1 medium onion, chopped
salt and pepper to taste
½ teaspoon dried thyme and rosemary mixed (or to taste)
1 bay leaf
3 strips fresh orange peel
4 tablespoons olive oil
2 cloves garlic, crushed
150 ml (¼ pint) dry white wine
50 g (2 oz) smoked streaky bacon
1 × 400 g (14 oz) can white beans
chopped parsley to garnish

Preparation time:	25 minutes plus marinating overnight and cooling
Cooking time:	50 minutes
Microwave setting:	High and conventional hob

White haricot beans, bacon, orange peel and garlic give a subtle flavour to tender lamb

—1—

Put the carrots into a bowl with two tablespoons water. Cover and microwave for 5 minutes. Drain and cool then mix with the onions, herbs, orange peel, oil, garlic and half the wine. Mix in the lamb then cover and marinate in the fridge overnight.

—2—

Next day, fry the bacon in a non-stick pan on top of the stove, until the bacon fat begins to run. Lift the meat out of the marinade and pat dry. Quickly fry the drained meat in the pan with the bacon until browned. Transfer the contents of the pan to a microwave-proof casserole dish.

—3—

Add the rest of the marinade and enough of the wine to cover. Cover and microwave for 20–25 minutes until the meat is tender.

Leave to cool. If possible leave overnight in the fridge for the flavours to develop.

—4—

Next day, stir in the drained beans, and microwave for 15 minutes. Remove the bay leaf and taste for seasoning. Sprinkle with parsley before serving.

Marseillaise Beef Casserole

Serves 6

750 g (1½ lb) frying steak, cut into even-sized squares
3 tablespoons olive oil
a few sprigs fresh rosemary
1 teaspoon dried thyme
2 cloves garlic, crushed
salt and pepper to taste
150 ml (¼ pint) red wine
12 button onions, peeled
100 g (4 oz) button mushrooms
1 tablespoon flour
150 ml (¼ pint) well-flavoured beef stock
a bouquet garni

Preparation time:	20 minutes, plus marinating overnight
Cooking time:	30 minutes, plus standing
Microwave setting:	High and conventional hob

Frying steak marinated with olive oil, herbs, garlic and wine for tenderness

—1—

Mix two tablespoons of the oil with the herbs, garlic, seasoning and red wine to make a marinade. Pour over the meat, mix well, then cover and refrigerate overnight.

—2—

Next day, heat the remaining oil in a frying pan on top of the stove. Fry the onions and mushrooms in the oil until golden brown, then transfer them to a microwave-proof casserole dish.

—3—

Lift the meat out of the marinade and pat dry. Brown quicky in the frying pan, then add to the casserole dish. Pour the juices from the frying pan into the jug. Stir in the flour. Microwave for 1 minute.

—4—

Stir in the marinade and stock. Cover and microwave for 6 minutes. Pour over the meat and vegetables.

—5—

Add the bouquet garni. Stir gently. Cover and microwave for 15 minutes, until the meat is tender. Taste for seasoning. Remove bouquet garni, then leave to stand for 5 minutes before serving.

French Beans with Ham

Serves 6

450 g (1 lb) fresh/frozen French beans, topped, tailed and halved
50 g (2 oz) unsalted butter
1 small onion, finely chopped
100 g (4 oz) good quality ham, cut in strips
salt and pepper to taste
8 stoned olives, halved

Preparation time:	10 minutes
Cooking time:	9–10 minutes plus standing
Microwave setting:	High

An attractive and tasty combination that's quick to make

—1—

Put the butter and onion in a medium-sized bowl and microwave for 3 minutes.

—2—

Add the beans, cover and microwave for 6–7 minutes until tender. Stir in the ham, seasoning and olives. Leave to stand for 3 minutes before serving.

Lapin Moutarde

Serves 4 to 6
1 rabbit, jointed
1 teaspoon salt
25 g (1 oz) lard or vegetable fat
1 medium onion, thinly sliced
1 tablespoon flour
2 tablespoons Dijon mustard
2 vegetable stock cubes dissolved in 450 ml
(¾ pint) boiling water
100 g (4 oz) green or yellow split peas, soaked in
cold water overnight
a sprig of fresh thyme
a bay leaf
salt and pepper to taste
To complete
6 rashers streaky bacon, rinded and halved
2 tablespoons croûtons
chopped parsley

Preparation time:	35 minutes plus soaking and freezing
Cooking time:	35–40 minutes plus reheating
Microwave setting:	High and conventional hob

An economical family meal with a hearty sauce. Chicken pieces can be substituted for the rabbit if you prefer them

—1—

Cover rabbit with warm water, add the salt and soak for 10 minutes. Remove from the water and dry with kitchen paper. Heat the fat in a large pan, brown the rabbit all over then place in a large bowl.

—2—

Add the onion to the pan and fry until golden. Stir in the flour, mustard and stock. Add to the rabbit with the drained split peas, thyme and bay leaf. Cover with pierced cling film and microwave for 15–20 minutes.

—3—

To complete: Remove rabbit pieces and process or liquidize the cooking liquid until smooth. Roll up the halved bacon rashers and thread on cocktail sticks. Microwave for 6 minutes.

—4—

Return the rabbit to the puréed sauce and microwave for 5 minutes. Serve on a warm dish, garnished with bacon rolls, croûtons and chopped parsley.

—5—

To freeze: Freeze without garnishes in a freezer/microwave-proof container.

—6—

To serve: Defrost in the microwave. Reheat on high power for 10–12 minutes. Transfer to a warmed serving dish and garnish as directed.

Chocolate Mocha Pots

Serves 6
175 g (6 oz) plain chocolate, chopped
2 teaspoons instant coffee power or granules
300 ml (½ pint) single cream
1 egg
½ teaspoon vanilla essence

Preparation time:	10 minutes plus chilling overnight
Cooking time:	2 minutes
Microwave setting:	High

A quick, easy and very rich end to a special meal

—1—

Put the chocolate and coffee powder/granules in a processor or blender. Put the cream into a jug and microwave for 2 minutes.

—2—

Pour in a steady stream on to the chocolate in the processor with the motor running. Process until smooth.

—3—

Add the egg and vanilla and process until smooth again. Pour into six small pots, glasses or ramekins and chill overnight.

Crab and Sweetcorn Soup

Serves 4 to 6

1.2 litres (2 pints) chicken stock, boiling hot
1 tablespoon sherry
1 teaspoon chopped fresh ginger
1 × 200 g (7 oz) can crabmeat, drained
1 × 275 g (9¾ oz) can creamed sweetcorn kernels
salt to taste
1 egg, beaten
a few drops sesame oil, to taste
1 tablespoon chopped spring onions to garnish
(optional)

Preparation time:	5 minutes
Cooking time:	7 minutes
Microwave setting:	High

The citrus-fresh taste of ginger enhances the flavour of the crabmeat in this simple soup

—1—

Put the stock, sherry, ginger, crabmeat and sweetcorn into a large bowl. Microwave for 6 minutes.

● Using your microwave creatively, it's possible to capture a variety of flavours and styles of cooking from around the world. Indian cooking has become increasingly popular, and need not be overpoweringly hot or too highly spiced, as you can adjust the spices to suit your palate.

● Chinese food is not all "sweet and sour" and sticky sauces. The microwave is perfect for cooking fish and vegetables the Chinese way, quickly sealing in flavours to preserve the fresh taste and the textures. And Mexican food doesn't mean "chillies with everything"! Many Mexican dishes interestingly combine creamy and crunchy textures, as well as hot and cool.

—2—

Stir in the salt, if needed. Pour in the egg in a steady stream, stirring constantly, followed by the sesame oil. Microwave for 1 minute. Garnish with chopped spring onions, and serve in warmed bowls.

Chinese Dinner

Crab and
 Sweetcorn
 Soup
Red-Cooked Pork
Broccoli with
 Sesame Seeds
Fish Fillets with
 Ginger and
 Garlic
Chinese Noodles

Crab and Sweetcorn Soup

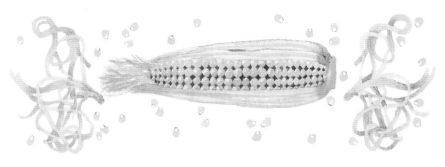

Red-Cooked Pork

Serves 4 to 6
1¼ kg (2½ lb) piece lean belly of pork
1 tablespoon caster sugar
1 teaspoon salt
1 tablespoon sherry
85 ml (3 fl oz) dark soy sauce
1 teaspoon finely chopped fresh root ginger
¼ teaspoon five spice powder
a few drops red food colouring (optional)
1 tablespoon runny honey

Preparation time:	10 minutes
Cooking time:	8 minutes plus standing
Microwave setting:	High

Chinese red-cooked meat is usually glazed with a mixture containing red food colouring to give the traditional appearance. The colouring is entirely optional, and if omitted doesn't alter the flavour

—1—

Cut the pork into 4 cm (1½ in) strips, discarding any bone. Lightly score the surface of the meat to absorb the marinade.

—2—

Mix together all the remaining ingredients, except for the honey. Put the meat into this marinade, rubbing it well into the cut surface. Place the meat on a ridged microwave dish or directly on to the rack or shelf in the microwave. Place a dish underneath to catch any drips.

—3—

Brush the meat with the honey, then microwave for 8 minutes. Brush again with honey, and leave to stand for 3 minutes before serving.

Broccoli with Sesame Seeds

Serves 4 to 6
450 g (1 lb) broccoli
1 tablespoon soya oil
1 tablespoon toasted sesame seeds
1 clove garlic, crushed
1 tablespoon soy sauce
1 teaspoon finely chopped fresh root ginger
salt and pepper to taste

Preparation time:	5 minutes
Cooking time:	11 minutes
Microwave setting:	High

For a special meal, add 50 g (2 oz) slivered almonds to the sauce with the broccoli

—1—

Cut the broccoli into florets and rinse well. Slice the stems lengthwise, then cut into 2½–4 cm (1–1½ in) slices.

—2—

Put the florets and sliced stems into a bowl with two tablespoons water and microwave for 8 minutes. Leave to stand while making the 'sauce'.

—3—

Put the remaining ingredients into another bowl and microwave for 3 minutes, stirring halfway through the cooking time. Toss the broccoli in the 'sauce' and serve piping hot.

Fish Fillets with Ginger and Garlic

Serves 4 to 6
350 g (12 oz) white fish fillets
1 teaspoon finely chopped fresh ginger
2 spring onions, shredded
2 cloves garlic, crushed
1 tablespoon black bean sauce
1 tablespoon dry sherry
1 teaspoon sesame oil

Preparation time: 5 minutes
Cooking time: 6 minutes plus standing
Microwave setting: High

Choose any white fish fillets, skinned. Cod, haddock, sole, plaice, halibut are all excellent for this simple but tasty low-calorie dish

—1—

Rinse and pat dry the fish fillets. Arrange in a single layer on a large, flat plate, suitable for serving. Sprinkle over the remaining ingredients.

—2—

Cover with polythene film* and microwave for 6 minutes. Leave to stand for 3 minutes before serving.

Chinese Noodles

Serves 4 to 6
1 × 250 g (8.82 oz) pack
Chinese egg noodles
100 g (4 oz) shelled prawns
a few drops sesame oil
2 teaspoons dry sherry
4 spring onions, finely chopped
1 clove garlic, crushed
2 tablespoons soya oil
4 Chinese dried mushrooms, soaked and stems removed
1 tablespoon light soy sauce
pinch of sugar
50 ml (2 fl oz) chicken or vegetable stock

Preparation time: 5 minutes
Cooking time: 10 minutes
Microwave setting: High and conventional hob

Chinese egg noodles are available from larger supermarkets and specialist food shops

—1—

Cook the noodles in plenty of boiling water on top of the stove according to the packet instructions. Drain. Meanwhile, marinate the prawns in the sesame oil and sherry.

—2—

Put the onions, garlic, soya oil and sliced soaked mushrooms in a large bowl. Microwave for 2 minutes.

—3—

Stir in the prawns and their marinade, the soy sauce, sugar and stock. Microwave for 1 minute. Stir this mixture into the drained noodles. Microwave for 3 minutes. Serve immediately.

Perfect Pasta

Serves 4
250 g (8 oz) dry pasta
1 teaspoon salt
1 tablespoon oil
1.7 litre (3 pt) boiling water

Preparation time: 5 minutes
Cooking time: 16 minutes
Microwave setting: High

The best way of cooking dry pasta in the microwave, using a 700 w cooker. (For 600 w cooker allow 15 seconds extra for every minute, for 500 w cooker allow 20 seconds extra for every minute)

—1—

Place all ingredients in a large bowl or oblong dish. Cover and cook for 8 minutes, stirring halfway through, and checking that all the pasta is under water. Then leave to stand for 8 minutes. (Tagliatelle, macaroni and vermicelli require only 4 minutes cooking time and 4 minutes standing time.)

—2—

Drain and then toss in butter. Add freshly-ground black pepper or some chopped parsley if liked. Serve on its own with Parmesan cheese or with a sauce.

Hints for cooking pasta
● Use a large quantity of boiling water.
● For best results use a large covered container for cooking lasagne.
● Most dry pastas will take about 8 minutes per 250 g (8 oz). Fresh pasta cooks in 1–1½ minutes.
● The pasta must be left to stand, a few minutes after cooking.

Lasagne

Serves 6
For the meat sauce
2 tablespoons olive oil
1 large onion, finely chopped
2 cloves garlic, crushed
450 g (1 lb) lean minced beef
1 tablespoon soya oil
1 tablespoon flour
1 × 400 g (14 oz) can tomatoes, drained
2 tablespoons tomato paste
2 teaspoons chopped parsley
2 teaspoons oregano
salt and pepper to taste
For the cheese sauce
600 ml (1 pt) milk
40 g (1½ oz) flour
40 g (1½ oz) butter or margarine
100 g (4 oz) grated mature
cheddar cheese
salt and pepper to taste
200 g (7 oz) lasagne, ready to use
To complete
75 g (3 oz) grated Cheddar cheese or a little
Parmesan

Preparation time:	20 minutes
Cooking time:	40–45 minutes
Microwave setting:	High and conventional hob and grill

—1—

For the meat sauce: Put the olive oil, onion and garlic into a large bowl. Cover and microwave for 3 minutes.

—2—

Fry the minced beef in the oil on top of the stove (or in a browning dish) until a good brown colour. Add to the onions with the rest of the ingredients listed for the meat sauce, using a fork to break up the tomatoes.

—3—

Cover the microwave for 8–10 minutes, stirring halfway through the cooking time.

—4—

For the cheese sauce: Put all the ingredients listed for the cheese sauce into a jug. Microwave for about 9 minutes or until thickened, stirring every 3 minutes.

—5—

To complete: Layer the pasta with the two sauces in a dish 25 by 20 cm (8 by 10 in) in the following order—meat/cheese sauce/pasta, finishing with cheese sauce. Microwave for 15 minutes.

—6—

Heat the grill. Sprinkle the remaining cheese over the lasagne and grill until golden and bubbling.

Three-Cheese Pizza

Serves 4 to 6
For the base
1 tablespoon olive oil
85 ml (3 fl oz) milk
2 teaspoons quick blend powdered yeast
175 g (6 oz) strong plain flour
large pinch of salt
For the topping
1 × 200 g (7 oz) can tomatoes,
drained and chopped
1 clove garlic, crushed
1 small onion, chopped
a pinch of sugar
¼ teaspoon dried oregano
25 g (1 oz) each finely chopped mozzarella,
dolcelatte and grated Parmesan

Preparation time:	25 minutes
Cooking time:	16 minutes
Microwave setting:	High and Defrost

Three well-known Italian cheeses – mozzarella, dolcelatte, and fresh Parmesan – make an unusual and delicious pizza topping

—1—

Put the oil and milk in a jug. Microwave on high power for 15 seconds. Sift the yeast with the flour and salt. Stir in the milk

mixture and mix to a soft dough. Knead for 10 minutes.

—2—

Pat or roll out to a circle about 30 cm (12 in) in diameter. Place on turntable base or a flat plate. Cover and microwave on defrost for 4 minutes until doubled in size. Cover while preparing the topping.

—3—

Put the tomatoes, garlic and onion in a bowl. Microwave on high power for 4 minutes, stirring halfway through the cooking time. Stir in the sugar, oregano and seasoning. Spread the topping over the dough base to within 2 cm (¾ in) of the edge. Sprinkle each cheese over a different third of the pizza. Microwave on high power for 8 minutes. Serve immediately.

Peperonata (p 114)

Mixed Seafood Salad

Serves 4 to 6

600 ml (1 pint) mussels, well scrubbed
8 tablespoons olive oil
2 tablespoons white wine
1 small onion, sliced
1 bay leaf
salt and pepper to taste
275 g (10 oz) squid, cleaned
4 scallops
175 g (6 oz) shelled prawns
3 tablespoons lemon juice
1 tablespoon capers
3 tablespoons chopped fresh parsley
1 clove garlic, crushed
black olives to garnish

Preparation time:	20 minutes plus cooling
Cooking time:	9 minutes
Microwave setting:	High

A wonderful first or main course of mussels, tender squid, scallops and prawns in olive oil

—1—

Discard any mussels that remain open when tapped, plus those with cracked shells, and any that float.

—2—

Put the cleaned mussels into a bowl with one tablespoon of the olive oil, the wine and two tablespoons water. Cover and microwave for 3 minutes, stirring halfway through the cooking time. The mussels are cooked when the shells open. Discard any with unopened shells. Remove the mussels from their shells and place in a serving dish.

—3—

Add 900 ml (1½ pints) boiling water, half the onion, the bay leaf and a little pepper to the mussel liquid left in the bowl. If the mussels are very salty you might not need to add extra salt. Add the squid to the liquid, then cover and microwave for 4 minutes until tender. Remove and cool the squid, then slice it into 5 mm (¼ in) strips.

—4—

Add the scallops to the cooking liquid in the bowl. Cover and microwave for 1½–2½ minutes until lightly poached. Drain, cool and slice if very large.

—5—

Put the scallops, squid and prawns into the serving dish containing the mussels. Mix together with the remaining oil, onion, lemon juice, caper, parsley and garlic. Taste before seasoning. Serve at room temperature, with a green salad.

Peperonata

Serves 4 to 6

2 tablespoons olive oil
1 large onion, chopped
1 each of large peppers, red,
green and yellow
1 tablespoon chopped parsley
1 clove garlic (or to taste), crushed
1 × 200 g (7 oz) can tomatoes, drained
salt and pepper to taste

Preparation time:	10 minutes
Cooking time:	14 minutes
Microwave setting:	High

—1—

Put the oil and onions in a large bowl. Core and thinly slice the peppers. Add to the bowl and mix well. Cover and microwave for 5 minutes, stirring twice during the cooking time.

Add the parsley and garlic to the mixture then microwave for 1 minute.

Stir in the tomatoes and seasoning to taste. Cover and microwave for 8 minutes, stirring halfway through the cooking time, until the peppers are very tender. Taste before serving. Serve piping hot, or cold, as a salad.

Pasticcio di Tagliatelle

Serves 4 to 6
450 g (1 lb) tagliatelle verde
75 g (3 oz) unsalted butter
175 g (6 oz) button mushrooms, sliced
1 clove garlic, crushed
75 g (3 oz) back bacon, diced
3 eggs, beaten
50 g (2 oz) each Gruyère and
ricotta cheese, cubed
50 g (2 oz) freshly grated Parmesan
150 ml (¼ pint) double cream
salt and black pepper to taste

Preparation time:	20 minutes
Cooking time:	20 minutes plus standing
Microwave setting:	High and conventional grill

A savoury dish of green tagliatelle noodles cooked with mushrooms, bacon, eggs and a mixture of cheeses

—1—

Cook the pasta, on top of the stove, according to the packet instructions. Do not overcook. Drain and toss in a warmed bowl with a third of the butter and seasoning to taste.

—2—

Put the rest of the butter, the mushrooms, garlic and bacon in another bowl. Cover and microwave for 5 minutes, stirring halfway through the cooking time. Stir in the eggs with a little seasoning.

—3—

Put half the pasta in the base of a large buttered microwave-proof serving dish. Spoon the mushroom and bacon mixture on top, then cover with the cubed Gruyère and ricotta. Sprinkle over half the Parmesan, then top with remaining pasta.

—4—

Pour over the cream and sprinkle with the remaining Parmesan. Microwave for 8 minutes. Leave to stand for 3 minutes then brown the top under a hot grill.

Granita di Caffe

Serves 4 to 6
100 g (4 oz) finely ground fresh coffee
75 g (3 oz) caster sugar
To serve
150 ml (¼ pint) whipping cream
1 tablespoon brandy (optional)

Preparation time:	5 minutes plus cooling and freezing
Cooking time:	1 minute
Microwave setting:	Medium

—1—

Put the coffee and sugar in a jug and microwave for 1 minute. Pour over 600 ml (1 pint) boiling water and stir well.

—2—

Leave the coffee to stand for 5 minutes. Stir again, then leave to cool.

—3—

Strain through a coffee filter or a sieve lined with kitchen paper. Freeze until mushy (about an hour). Stir through lightly with a fork to break up the ice crystals, then return to the freezer until firm.

—4—

Spoon the granita into chilled glasses and top with the whipped cream, flavoured with the brandy.

Chicken with Hot Pepper Sauce

Serves 4–6

4 boneless chicken breasts, skinned
1 tablespoon oil
15 g (½ oz) butter
1 large onion, thinly sliced
1 fresh chilli, seeded and chopped
1½ green peppers, cored and sliced
salt and pepper to taste
50 ml (2 fl oz) milk
85 ml (3 fl oz) double cream
½ small red repper, cored and sliced
½ small yellow pepper, cored and sliced

Preparation time:	20 minutes
Cooking time:	20 minutes
Microwave setting:	High and conventional hob

You can add an extra chilli for extra flavour, or omit it altogether – this dish will still taste delicious

—1—

Quickly fry the chicken breasts in the hot oil and butter, on top of the stove, until browned on both sides. Lift out, draining well, and place in a shallow microwave-proof dish. Add the onion to the frying pan and cook until soft and golden. Transfer to a bowl.

—2—

Meanwhile process the chilli with one green pepper, a little seasoning, the milk and cream. Stir this mixture into the onions with the remaining pepper slices. Microwave for 2 minutes.

—3—

Spoon this mixture over the chicken breasts. Microwave for 12 minutes or until the chicken is thoroughly cooked. Serve immediately.

Peppered Rice Casserole

Serves 4–6

2 tablespoons soya oil
1 clove garlic, crushed
175 g (6 oz) long grain rice
450 ml (¾ pint) boiling chicken stock
½ small onion, finely chopped
1 green chilli
150 ml (¼ pint) soured cream
salt and pepper to taste
75 g (3 oz) mature Cheddar cheese, grated
75 g (3 oz) mozzarella cheese, sliced
1 red and 1 green pepper, cored and sliced
1 × 1.7 litre (3 pint) casserole dish, greased

Preparation time:	10 minutes
Cooking time:	24 minutes plus standing
Microwave setting:	High

This tasty rice dish would make a lovely supper served with a green salad

—1—

Put the oil in a large bowl with the garlic. Microwave for 30 seconds.

—2—

Stir in the rice, stock, onion, and the whole chilli. Cover and microwave for 12 minutes. Stand for 5 minutes then remove chilli.

—3—

Layer the rice in the casserole dish with the cream, cheeses and peppers. Season each layer and finish with a layer of cheese.

—4—

Microwave for 10–12 minutes. Leave to stand for 3 minutes.

● If food 'pops' in the microwave, it is due to an excessive build-up of steam inside vessels and membranes, and certain foods which have a high protein content.
● Try reducing the power, but remember to increase the cooking time.
● It is worth while covering food, even though it may only be in the oven for a minute or so.
● Remember to score the skin on fish and pierce food items such as kidneys.

Corn and Courgettes

Serves 4–6
2 corn-on-the-cob
1 small onion
½ green chilli, seeded and chopped
25 g (1 oz) butter or margarine
350 g (12 oz) courgettes, wiped and sliced
salt and pepper to taste
chopped parsley to garnish

Preparation time:	10 minutes
Cooking time:	10–13 minutes
Microwave setting:	High

A colourful combination of summer vegetables

—1—

Trim the corn cobs, if necessary, to remove the husks. Cut the cobs into 2 cm (¾ in) rounds. Put the onion, green chilli and butter into a large bowl. Microwave for 5 minutes.

—2—

Stir in the corn, courgettes, three tablespoons water and seasonings to taste. Cover and microwave for 5–8 minutes until the corn is tender, stirring halfway through the cooking time. Taste for seasoning, adjusting if necessary, then serve.

Tacos filled with Chilli Beef Sauce

Serves 4–6

2 tablespoons soya oil
1 large onion, finely chopped
1 green chilli, seeded and chopped
½ red pepper, cored and diced
2 cloves garlic, crushed
1 tablespoon chilli powder (or to taste)
1 teaspoon ground coriander
2 teaspoons ground cumin
1 teaspoon dried oregano
450 g (1 lb) minced lean beef
6 tablespoons tomato purée
150 ml (¼ pint) beef or vegetable stock
2 × 400 g (14 oz) cans red kidney beans
salt to taste
8 taco shells

Preparation time:	20 minutes plus chilling overnight
Cooking time:	25 minutes
Microwave setting:	High and conventional hob

Ready-made taco shells can be found in large supermarkets. Serve gently warmed

—1—

Heat the oil in a frying pan on top of the stove, add the onion and cook until soft and golden brown. Add the chilli, red pepper and garlic. Fry for 2 minutes, then stir in the spices and stir-fry for 1 minute. Transfer the mixture to a microwave-proof casserole dish.

—2—

Quickly fry the mince in the frying pan until browned, then add to the casserole. Stir in the tomato purée and stock. Cover and microwave for 10 minutes.

—3—

Stir well, then add the drained beans. Microwave for 5 minutes. (If possible, leave to cool at this point, then chill overnight, to allow the flavours to develop. Reheat on high power until the mixture has thoroughly boiled, adding a little extra stock as necessary.)

—4—

When ready to serve, spoon the meat sauce into the taco shells and and microwave for 3 minutes. If wished, serve with soured cream, plain rice and salad.

Variation

Skinned peppers have a milder, sweeter flavour. To remove the skins, halve the peppers then grill the skin side until the skin bubbles and turns dark brown. Wrap in a damp tea-towel until cool, then peel off charred skin.

Richly-Flavoured Spinach

Serves 4 to 6

1 small onion, finely chopped
2 tablespoons soya oil
½ green chilli, seeded and chopped
½ in piece fresh ginger, peeled and chopped
1 clove garlic, crushed
455 g (1 lb) packet frozen leaf spinach
2 tablespoons lemon juice
½ teaspoon garam masala
salt to taste

Preparation time:	10 minutes
Cooking time:	14 minutes
Microwave setting:	High

Chilli, fresh ginger and spices are unusual but excellent additions to frozen spinach

—1—

Put the onion, oil, chilli, ginger and garlic into a medium-sized bowl. Microwave, uncovered, on 'high' for 4 minutes, stirring after 2 minutes. Add the frozen spinach. Cover and cook on 'high' for 7 minutes, stirring occasionally to break up the spinach.

—2—

Stir in the lemon juice and garam masala. Microwave on 'high' for 1 minute. Taste for seasoning, adding salt as necessary. Serve immediately.

Mogul Chicken

Serves 4 to 6
4 to 6 chicken joints
2 in piece of fresh ginger
2 cloves garlic
1 green chilli, seeds removed
½ teaspoon salt
140 ml (¼ pt) single cream
280 ml (½ pt) natural yogurt
1 teaspoon saffron strands
3 tablespoons soya oil
450 g (1 lb) onions, peeled and chopped
100 g (4 oz) blanched almonds
140 ml (¼ pt) chicken or vegetable stock

Preparation time:	10 minutes
Cooking time:	20–25 minutes plus marinating
Microwave setting:	High

Chicken in an almond-rich, creamy sauce delicately spiced with fresh ginger and chilli

—1—

Remove the skin from the chicken. Peel and chop the ginger. Using a food processor or blender, grind to a paste the ginger, garlic, chilli and salt with one tablespoon water. Rub this paste into the chicken pieces and leave to marinate for 30 minutes. Meanwhile mix the cream with the yogurt and saffron and leave to stand for 20 minutes. Then pour this mixture over the paste-coated chicken and mix well. Cover and refrigerate overnight.

—2—

Next day, heat the oil in a pan on top of the stove. Add the onion and fry until golden. Transfer the onions to a large microwave-proof dish, add the chicken and its marinade and mix well. Cover and microwave on 'high' for 10 to 12 minutes.

—3—

Meanwhile grind or process the almonds until fine. Stir into the chicken mixture with the stock. Microwave, uncovered, on 'high' for a further 10 to 15 minutes. The exact time will depend on the size of the chicken pieces, the dish, etc.

—4—

To test if the chicken is cooked, stick a skewer or sharp knife into each piece; if the juices run clear the chicken is cooked. If the juices are pink, return to the microwave for a couple of minutes more. Taste for seasoning before serving.

Special Rice Pilau

Serves 4 to 6
340 g (12 oz) basmati rice
1 onion, finely chopped
1 tablespoon soya oil
1 clove garlic, crushed
1 green chilli, seeded and chopped
1 in piece root ginger, peeled and chopped
1 teaspoon salt
2 teaspoons garam masala
600 ml (1 pt) chicken or vegetable stock

Preparation time:	15 minutes
Cooking time:	about 30 minutes
Microwave setting:	High

—1—

Wash and drain the rice. Put the onion and oil into a bowl, cover and microwave on 'high' for 4 minutes, stirring halfway through the cooking time.

—2—

Then add the garlic, chilli, ginger, salt and garam masala. Mix well and microwave on 'high' uncovered for 2 minutes. Stir in the rice. Microwave on 'high' for 1 minute uncovered. Add the stock, stir well, then cover and microwave on 'high' for 12 minutes. Leave to stand, covered, for 10 minutes before serving.

Indian Menu
Richly-Flavoured
   Spinach
Mogul Chicken
Special Rice
   Pilau

*Alternative
Christmas Pudding
(p 126)*

Catering for Christmas cheer

CHRISTMAS MENU

The festive season is one of the many times when a microwave will let you prepare some recipes ahead and cook others, like the traditional Christmas pudding, in a fraction of the time. We have devised here an easy yet delicious Christmas dinner cooked entirely by microwave. This doesn't mean that you should totally abandon your conventional cooker — it will still be invaluable for keeping everything warm, making gravy and cooking additional vegetables if required. Although the method of defrosting a turkey is included, it is still preferable to defrost large turkeys slowly in the fridge.

Old-Fashioned Punch

2 litres (3½ pints) of red wine
1 × 10 cm (4 in) cinnamon stick
2 cloves
1 teaspoon ground mixed spice
2 oranges
225 g (8 oz) loaf sugar, rubbed
over oranges
grated rind of 1 lemon
16 cl bottle brandy

Preparation time:	5 minutes
Cooking time:	6–7 minutes
Microwave setting:	High

The traditional drink made in a thoroughly modern way!

—1—

Put all the ingredients except the brandy in a large microwave-proof bowl. Microwave for 6–7 minutes to heat through, removing the spices after 3 minutes.

—2—

Stir in the brandy and serve while piping hot. This punch can be easily reheated in the microwave for latecomers, either as a whole or in individual glasses.

Traditional-Style Turkey

1 × 4½ kg (10 lb) turkey (see recipe)
watercress to garnish

Preparation time:	5 minutes plus defrosting if necessary
Cooking time:	1 hour 10 minutes plus standing
Microwave setting:	Defrost (for frozen turkey) and High

—1—

To thaw by microwave pierce the plastic freezer wrapper and remove the metal clip. The wing and leg tips can be shielded with foil. Defrost for about 10–12 minutes per lb on defrost or low setting – see your manufacturer's guide. During defrosting turn the bird over twice, and pour off any liquid in the plastic wrappers and remove the giblets as soon as they loosen. Complete the defrosting at room temperature or by immersing the bird in its plastic wrapper in a bowl of cold water. Pat dry, inside and out, with paper towels and cook immediately.

—2—

Cover the wings and legs with small pieces of foil. Cover the turkey completely with cling film, and stand in a shallow dish.

—3—

Microwave on high power for 1 hour 10 minutes. (Turkey needs 7–8 minutes per 1 lb for a bird up to 12 lb. A larger bird will not fit into the average microwave.)

—4—

Remove the turkey from the microwave and remove the cling film. Cover completely with foil and leave to stand for 25–30 minutes in a warm place.

Cranberry Sauce

Serves 6 to 8
350 g (12 oz) cranberries
50 g (2 oz) caster sugar, or to taste
grated rind and juice of 1 orange
a small knob of butter

Preparation time:	5 minutes
Cooking time:	5–7 minutes, plus standing
Microwave setting:	High

—1—

Place the cranberries in a bowl with the sugar, orange rind and juice. Cover and microwave for 5–7 minutes.

—2—

Stir in the knob of butter and taste, adding more sugar if necessary. Stand, covered, until ready to serve.

● Always cover turkeys loosely during thawing to retain moisture.
● Pour off any accumulated liquid during thawing.
● Wrap any bone showing – wing tips, end of drumsticks etc. in small pieces of foil for at least half the cooking time. If warm spots occur, cover these with foil.

Sausage and Cranberry Stuffing

1 onion, finely chopped
1 stick celery, finely sliced
25 g (1 oz) butter or margarine, melted
3 tablespoons Orange Cranberry Sauce
the liver from the turkey, roughly chopped
75 g (3 oz) fresh breadcrumbs
225 g (8 oz) good quality sausagemeat
2 tablespoons chopped fresh parsley
salt, pepper and paprika to taste

Preparation time:	10 minutes
Cooking time:	8–10 minutes plus standing
Microwave setting:	High

A moist, tasty stuffing flavoured with ready-made Orange Cranberry Sauce

—1—

Put all the ingredients into a bowl and mix well. Spoon into a shallow serving dish. Microwave for 8–10 minutes.

—2—

Leave to stand for 2–3 minutes, then serve.

Apricot and Chestnut Stuffing

50 g (2 oz) fresh spinach, washed
175 g (6 oz) fresh wholemeal breadcrumbs
50 g (2 oz) cooked whole chestnuts, chopped
50 g (2 oz) dried apricots, ready-soaked and chopped
50 g (2 oz) large seedless California raisins
salt, pepper and cayenne to taste
¼ teaspoon ground cinnamon
1 egg, beaten

Preparation time:	15 minutes
Cooking time:	7 minutes plus standing
Microwave setting:	High

Unusual, fruity and excellent with goose, duck or turkey

—1—

Put the spinach into a heavy-duty polythene bag or a special microwave cook bag. Fold the end under, then microwave for 2 minutes.

—2—

When cool enough to handle, squeeze the spinach to remove the excess liquid, then chop roughly.

—3—

Mix the spinach with the remaining ingredients and spoon into a shallow microwave-proof serving dish. Microwave for 5 minutes.

—4—

Leave to stand for a minute or two then serve.

Sage and Onion Stuffing Balls

25 g (1 oz) butter or margarine
1 medium onion, finely chopped
2 tablespoons chopped fresh parsley
1 tablespoon dried sage
the grated rind of 1 lemon
salt and pepper to taste
175 g (6 oz) fresh white breadcrumbs

Preparation time:	10 minutes
Cooking time:	8–10 minutes
Microwave setting:	High

—1—

Put the butter or margarine and the onion into a mixing bowl. Microwave for 3–4 minutes until softened.

—2—

Stir in the remaining ingredients. Roll the mixture into even-sized balls and microwave for 5–6 minutes.

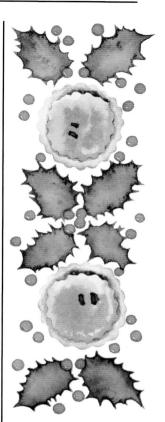

Creamy Bread Sauce

6 cloves
1 small onion, peeled
300 ml (½ pint) milk
6 peppercorns
a bay leaf
75 g (3 oz) fresh white breadcrumbs
50 g (2 oz) butter
salt, pepper and nutmeg to taste
2 tablespoons single cream

Preparation time:	10 minutes
Cooking time:	8 minutes
Microwave setting:	High

—1—

Push the cloves into the onion, then put into a jug with the milk, peppercorns and bay leaf. Cover with pierced cling film. Microwave for 5 minutes. Leave to stand for at least 30 minutes, then discard the flavourings.

—2—

Stir in the breadcrumbs and butter, then season to taste.

—3—

Pour into a serving jug. Cover and microwave for 3 minutes, stirring halfway through. Stir in the cream and leave to stand for 3–4 minutes before serving.

Gratin of Brussels Sprouts

1 kg (2 lb) Brussels sprouts, trimmed
For the sauce
25 g (1 oz) butter or margarine
25 g (1 oz) flour
450 ml (¾ pint) hot milk
4 tablespoons single cream
100 g (4 oz) cheese, grated (Cheddar or Gruyère)
salt, pepper, nutmeg and mustard to taste
For the topping
3 tablespoons dry breadcrumbs
2 tablespoons Parmesan cheese, grated

Preparation time:	10 minutes plus cooling
Cooking time:	24–28 minutes
Microwave setting:	High and conventional grill

—1—

Put the sprouts into a large bowl with three tablespoons water. Cover with cling film and microwave for 7–9 minutes, depending on size, until tender. Rinse with cold water, then drain thoroughly. Put into a microwave-proof serving dish.

—2—

Put the butter into a jug. Microwave for 1 minute. Stir in the flour and milk. Cover with cling film and microwave for 6 minutes, stirring every 2 minutes. Stir in the cream and the cheese. Season well. Pour the sauce over the sprouts. Leave to cool.

Mix the breadcrumbs with the Parmesan and sprinkle over the sprouts. Microwave for 10–12 minutes until thoroughly heated. Place under a hot grill for a few moments to brown top.

Amandine Potatoes

750 g (1½ lb) potatoes, peeled
salt and pepper to taste
40 g (1½ oz) butter
2 tablespoons milk
1 egg, beaten
100 g (4 oz) blanched almonds, finely chopped
and toasted

Preparation time: 15 minutes plus
chilling
Cooking time: 12–14 minutes
Microwave setting: High

Cut up the potatoes into even-sized pieces. Put into a large bowl with a pinch of salt and 4 tablespoons water. Cover and microwave for 9–10 minutes.

Leave to stand for 5 minutes. Mash until completely smooth, then beat in the butter and milk, and plenty of seasoning. Chill for at least 30 minutes.

Roll the mixture into golfball-sized pieces. Coat each ball thoroughly in beaten egg and then in the chopped almonds. Chill until needed.

Put the potatoes on to a plate or tray lined with kitchen paper and lightly prick with a fork or cocktail stick. Microwave for 3–4 minutes until piping hot.

Citrus Glazed Gammon

1 kg (2 lb) piece smoked pork loin
15 g (½ oz) butter or margarine
10 g (¼ oz) soft dark brown sugar
½ orange
1 lemon
2 teaspoons marmalade
1 teaspoon cornflour

Preparation time: 10 minutes
Cooking time: 55–57 minutes
Microwave setting: High, then Medium

Serve hot with our tangy sauce, or cold, thinly sliced, with crisp salads for Boxing Day lunch

Score a lattice pattern on the rind of the gammon using the tip of a sharp knife. Put the butter into a small dish. Microwave on high power for 30 seconds or until melted. Mix in the sugar. Put the meat into a shallow dish and spoon over the butter and sugar mixture. Microwave on medium power for 5 minutes.

Meanwhile, thinly peel the rind from the orange and lemon, and slice into fine shreds. Squeeze the juice from the fruit and reserve. Remove the meat from the microwave. Arrange a few of the orange and lemon shreds in the scored lattice of the gammon rind.

Microwave on medium power for a further 45 minutes until the meat is cooked right through. Brush with the marmalade.

Mix the cornflour to a paste with a little cold water. Stir in 150 ml (¼ pint) water, the fruit juices, and any meat juices which have collected during cooking. Microwave the sauce on medium power for 5–7 minutes, stirring occasionally. Stir in the remaining orange and lemon shreds and serve in a sauce boat.

● Microwaving your Christmas pudding on the day is an enormous time saver for the frantic cook.
● The pudding can be reheated on its serving dish and the alcohol for the flaming ceremony can also be warmed through in the microwave – do not set alight in the microwave.

Microwave Christmas Pudding

Makes 1 pudding
175 g (6 oz) currants
175 g (6 oz) sultanas
175 g (6 oz) large raisins
40 g (1½ oz) candied peel
75 g (3 oz) carrot, scrubbed and grated
grated rind of 1 lime
100 g (4 oz) soft dark brown sugar
75 g (3 oz) sunflower seeds, toasted
40 g (1½ oz) fresh breadcrumbs
100 g (4 oz) shredded suet
½ teaspoon each nutmeg, mixed spice
and cinnamon
75 g (3 oz) plain flour
3 eggs, beaten
1 tablespoon black treacle
6 tablespoons brandy or sherry
1 × 1.5 litre (2½ pint) pudding
basin, lightly greased

Preparation time:	10 minutes plus cooling
Cooking time:	10–12 minutes plus reheating
Microwave setting:	High

—1—

Thoroughly wash and dry the fruit. Chop the candied peel (with a little of the flour). Put all these ingredients into a bowl with the lime rind, sugar, sunflower seeds, breadcrumbs and suet. Mix them well.

—2—

Sift together the flour and spices and stir in. Beat the eggs with the treacle and brandy then mix into the other ingredients. When thoroughly blended, spoon into the basin. Cover with cling film and microwave for 10–12 minutes until firm. Cool, then wrap and store in a cool, dry place.

—3—

To reheat: Microwave for 4–7 minutes until piping hot. Serve with cream, brandy butter or with brandy white sauce.

The Alternative Christmas Pudding

50 g (2 oz) butter or margarine
50 g (2 oz) soft dark brown sugar
2 crisp eating apples, peeled and chopped
25 g (1 oz) walnuts, chopped
1 dried banana, chopped
100 g (4 oz) currants, washed and dried
25 g (1 oz) chopped mixed peel
3 teaspoons mixed spice
For the sponge
175 g (6 oz) butter or margarine
175 g (6 oz) soft light brown sugar
2 eggs, beaten
1 tablespoon treacle
2 tablespoons orange juice
225 g (8 oz) self-raising flour
grated rind of 1 orange
For the sauce
juice of 2 large oranges (to
measure 150 ml/¼ pint)
finely grated rind of 1 orange
1 teaspoon cornflour
2 tablespoons golden syrup
1 tablespoon black treacle
1 × 1.5 litre (2½ pint) pudding
basin, greased and base-lined

Preparation time:	25 minutes
Cooking time:	16–20 minutes
Microwave setting:	High

—1—

Put the butter and sugar into a bowl and microwave for 1½–2 minutes or until the butter has melted. Stir, then stir in the chopped fruits, nuts, peel and spice.

—2—

Cream the butter and sugar, slowly beat in the eggs, treacle and orange juice. Fold in the flour and orange rind. Spoon a little sponge mixture on to the base of the basin and top with layer of fruit. Continue with layers of sponge and fruit, finishing with a layer of sponge. Cover the basin loosely with cling film and microwave for 12–15 minutes, or until the sponge is cooked through.

—3—

In a jug blend a little orange juice with the

grated rind and cornflour to make a smooth paste. Slowly stir in the remaining ingredients. Cover with cling film and microwave for 2–3 minutes, stirring occasionally until slightly thickened.

—4—

Turn the pudding on to a large plate and drizzle a little of the sauce over the top and sides to coat. Serve the remaining sauce separately.

Spiced Exotic Fruit Salad

1 small pineapple, peeled
1 ripe mango, peeled
2 pink grapefruit, peeled
3 bananas, peeled
2 tablespoons large California raisins
1 tablespoon rum (optional)
2 tablespoons hazelnuts or
almonds, toasted
50 g (2 oz) unsalted butter
50 g (2 oz) soft light brown sugar
1–2 teaspoons mild curry powder

Preparation time: 10 minutes
Cooking time: 4–5 minutes
Microwave setting: High

An unusual, Caribbean-style dessert of fresh fruit and nuts that tastes out of this world

—1—

Cut the pineapple into chunks, discarding the core. Dice the mango, segment the grapefruit and cut the bananas diagonally into slices. Soak the raisins in the rum if using.

—2—

Put the butter, sugar and curry powder into a large microwave-proof serving bowl. Microwave mixture for 2 minutes, stirring after 1 minute.

—3—

Stir in the remaining ingredients. Microwave for 2–3 minutes, stirring frequently, until piping hot.

—4—

Serve immediately with vanilla ice cream – delicious!

Brandy Butter

Serves 6 to 8
175 g (6 oz) unsalted butter
75 g (3 oz) icing sugar, sifted
75 g (3 oz) caster sugar
2–3 tablespoons brandy

Preparation time: 5 minutes
Cooking time: 30 seconds
Microwave setting: High

Keep some in the freezer for a special treat during the year

—1—

Place the butter in a bowl and microwave for 30 seconds to soften.

—2—

Beat until soft and creamy then gradually beat in the sugars, followed by the brandy.

—3—

Spoon into a serving dish and chill until ready to serve.

Variation
Soft light brown sugar can be used instead of icing and caster sugar.

Iced Summer Fruit Bombe (p 131); Ragoût of Beef (p 130); Red Mullet Ramekins (p 130)

Freezer and microwave – good companions

FROZEN ASSETS

If you have owned a freezer for years but have only recently acquired a microwave, you're probably wondering how you ever managed without it, as the freezer and microwave make such an ideal kitchen team. Vegetables can be transferred from the freezer to the microwave and cooked from frozen in minutes. Meals can be prepared ahead, cooked in the microwave, then frozen. When you next need a speedy hot meal, just pop it into the microwave. If you use your freezer to buy food in bulk and store produce when it is cheap, the microwave will then add speed and adaptability when it comes to thawing and cooking your handy frozen assets.

Red Mullet Ramekins

Serves 4
2 red mullet, weighing about 450 g (1 lb)
100 g (4 oz) butter
1 small onion or shallot, finely chopped
1 tablespoon chopped parsley
1 clove garlic, crushed
juice of ½ lemon
salt, pepper and cayenne to taste
To complete
a few sprigs of fresh dill
1 × 275 g (10 oz) can consommé
4 ramekins or a small microwave-proof terrine

Preparation time:	25 minutes plus chilling and freezing
Cooking time:	6–8 minutes
Microwave setting:	High

—1—

Gut the mullet, taking care not to remove the liver, which is considered a delicacy and adds to the special flavour of this fish.

—2—

Place on a microwave-proof plate, cover loosely with cling film and microwave for 6–8 minutes.

—3—

Cool slightly and remove the skin and bones. Process or pound the flesh and liver with the butter, onion, parsley, garlic and lemon juice until smooth. Season to taste. Spoon into the dishes and level the surface.

—4—

To complete: Pour 2–3 tablespoons consommé over each pâté and chill until almost set. Arrange sprigs of dill in the consommé and chill to set completely.

—5—

To freeze: Freeze before topping with consommé.

—6—

To serve: Defrost overnight in the fridge. Cover with consommé and decorate as directed.

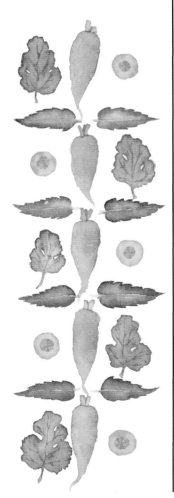

Ragoût of Beef with Carrots and Fennel

Serves 6
750 g (1½ lb) frying steak
2 tablespoons oil
12 button onions, peeled
1 tablespoon flour
1 clove garlic, crushed
150 ml (¼ pint) red wine
300 ml (½ pint) canned beef consommé
1 bouquet garni
salt and pepper to taste
225 g (8 oz) carrots, peeled
1 bulb fennel, trimmed and finely sliced
finely shredded rind of 1 lime

Preparation time:	30 minutes plus freezing
Cooking time:	32–34 minutes plus standing and reheating
Microwave setting:	High and conventional hob

Frying steak is used as the short cooking time keeps it tender and full of flavour

—1—

Trim the meat and cut into 5 cm (2 in) pieces. Heat the oil in a large frying pan and quickly brown the meat all over. Use a slotted spoon to transfer it to a microwave-proof dish. Add the onions to the pan, roll them around until they begin to colour, and add to the meat.

—2—

Pour the pan juices into a jug and stir in the flour. Microwave for 1 minute. Stir in the garlic, red wine and consommé. Cover and microwave for 6 minutes, stirring every 2 minutes.

—3—

Pour over the meat and add the bouquet garni. Cover and microwave for 15 minutes until the meat is tender. Season to taste and leave to stand, covered.

—4—

Meanwhile, cut the carrots into matchsticks and place in a bowl with the fennel and 4 tablespoons water. Cover and microwave for 8–10 minutes until tender. Drain.

—5—

Pour a little boiling water over the lime shreds to blanch them. Drain. Remove the bouquet garni from the ragoût and top with the carrots and fennel. Scatter over the lime shreds and serve with baked jacket potatoes, or noodles tossed in butter.

—6—

To freeze: Freeze the ragoût and vegetables separately.

—7—

To serve: Defrost ragoût and vegetables in the microwave. Arrange the carrots and fennel on top of the meat, cover and microwave on high power for 12–15 minutes until heated through. Garnish with lime shreds.

Iced Summer Fruit Bombe

Serves 8
For the fruit sorbet
225 g (8 oz) fresh or frozen blackcurrants
75 g (3 oz) granulated sugar
2 tablespoons lemon juice
For the ice cream
300 ml (½ pint) milk
4 egg yolks
100 g (4 oz) caster sugar
300 ml (½ pint) double cream, lightly whipped
1 teaspoon vanilla essence
To decorate
frosted blackcurrants (see recipe below)
1 × 1.5 litre (2½ pint) bombe mould or basin

Preparation time:	35 minutes, plus freezing
Cooking time:	8–9 minutes
Microwave setting:	Defrost, then High

We used blackcurrants for our bombe but any combination of fruits, will work equally well

—1—

Thaw frozen fruit on defrost in the microwave. Purée the fruit in a processor or liquidizer, and sieve to remove any stalks or pips.

—2—

Place the sugar in a jug with 150 ml (¼ pint) water. Microwave on high power for 4 minutes, stirring every minute. Allow to cool. When cold stir into the purée with the lemon juice. Pour into a freezer container and freeze until slushy. Beat well (easily done in a mixer or processor) until smooth, then return to the freezer until soft enough to spoon.

—3—

Meanwhile chill the mould or basin. Coat the base and sides of the mould with the fruit sorbet and freeze until firm.

—4—

For the ice cream: Heat the milk in a jug for 1 minute on high power. Whisk the yolks and sugar together until pale. Pour on the milk; mix well. Return to the jug and microwave on high power for 3–4 minutes, stirring every minute. The custard will thicken, but don't allow to overcook or it will curdle. Strain and leave to cool.

—5—

Fold the cream and vanilla essence into the cooled custard. Freeze until slushy, then beat in a mixer. Spoon into the bombe, cover and freeze.

—6—

About half an hour before serving, unmould the bombe by briefly dipping in warm water, or wrapping a hot cloth around the outside. Leave in the fridge.

—7—

To frost fruit: Dip washed, dried fruit into broken-up egg white, then in caster sugar, and use to decorate the bombe.

Celery and Blue Cheese Soup

Serves 6 to 8
50 g (2 oz) butter or margarine
175 g (6 oz) onions, finely chopped
225 g (8 oz) celery, sliced
1 clove garlic, crushed
2 tablespoons flour
450 ml (¾ pint) chicken stock
150 ml (¼ pint) vermouth or extra chicken stock
450 ml (¾ pint) milk
150 g (5 oz) blue cheese, diced
salt and pepper to taste
to serve
4 tablespoons cream
a few celery tops

Preparation time:	15 minutes plus freezing
Cooking time:	11–12 minutes plus reheating
Microwave setting:	High

—1—

Put the butter into a large bowl. Microwave for 40–60 seconds until melted and hot. Add the onions, celery and garlic. Microwave for 2–3 minutes, stirring occasionally.

—2—

Stir in the flour, followed by the liquids. Microwave for 8 minutes or until the vegetables are tender. Strain off the liquid and reserve.

—3—

Purée the vegetables with the cheese and a little of the reserved liquid. Stir this mixture back into the remaining liquid and season to taste.

—4—

To freeze: Allow to cool completely. Pour into a rigid freezer container and freeze for up to three months.

Beef with Cranberries and Walnuts

Serves 6
2 sticks celery, thinly sliced
1 medium onion, finely chopped
1 clove garlic, crushed
3 tablespoons soya oil
750 g (1½ lb) topside beef, cubed
15 g (½ oz) plain flour
grated rind of 1 orange
1 tablespoon chopped fresh parsley
¼ teaspoon dried mixed herbs
½ teaspoon each ground cinnamon and ginger
a pinch ground cloves
salt and pepper
1 teaspoon French mustard
250 ml (8 fl oz) claret
4 tablespoons port
175 g (6 oz) cranberries, thawed if necessary
100 g (4 oz) bottled cranberry sauce
25 g (1 oz) walnut pieces
To complete
25 g (1 oz) walnut pieces
1 tablespoon chopped fresh parsley

Preparation time:	20 minutes plus freezing
Cooking time:	1 hour 10 minutes
Microwave setting:	High, then Defrost

—1—

Quickly fry the celery and onions in two tablespoons oil, on top of the stove. When lightly browned add the garlic and cook gently for 1 minute. Transfer to a large bowl.

—2—

Fry the meat in the remaining oil to seal and brown. Add to the vegetables in the bowl. Cover and microwave on high power for 10 minutes, stirring halfway through the cooking time.

—3—

Add the flour, grated orange rind, herbs, spices, salt and pepper. Stir in the mustard, claret and port. When well-mixed, cover and microwave on high power for 10 minutes. Add the cranberries and cranberry sauce. Microwave on defrost (or low power) for 50 minutes.

—4—

Stir in the walnut pieces and microwave on defrost (or low power) for a further 5 minutes. Cool, then spoon into two rigid containers and freeze for up to six months.

—5—

To use from frozen: Thaw each container in the microwave on defrost for 40 minutes. Reheat on high power for 4–5 minutes until thoroughly boiled. Serve garnished with chopped parsley and walnuts.

Wholegrain Pilaff

Serves 6

25 g (1 oz) butter or margarine
1 medium onion, finely chopped
225 g (8 oz) long grain brown rice
600 ml (1 pint) boiling chicken or vegetable stock
75 g (3 oz) button mushrooms, sliced
2 teaspoons toasted sesame seeds
salt and pepper to taste

Preparation time:	10 minutes plus freezing
Cooking time:	39–44 minutes plus standing and reheating
Microwave setting:	High

—1—

Put the butter and onion in a large bowl or microwave-proof casserole, and microwave for 3 minutes until softened. Stir in the rice and microwave for 1 minute. Add the boiling stock, cover and microwave for 30 minutes.

—2—

Stir in the mushrooms and microwave for 5–10 minutes until the mushrooms are tender, the rice is cooked and all the liquid has been absorbed. Stir in the sesame seeds and season to taste. Cover and leave to stand for 4 minutes, then serve.

—3—

To freeze: Spoon into a freezer container. Cool and freeze for up to 6 months. To use from frozen: Thaw and reheat by cooking on high power for 10–12 minutes.

Iced Gâteau St Clements (p 135); Pork Fillet Normande (p 134); Celery and Blue Cheese Soup; Three-Vegetable Mash (p 134); Wholegrain Pilaff; Beef with Cranberries and Walnuts

Pork Fillet Normande

Serves 4
1 tablespoon soya oil
450 g (1 lb) pork fillet
25 g (1 oz) butter
1 medium onion, finely chopped
2 tablespoons flour
65 ml (2½ fl oz) dry cider
150 ml (¼ pint) chicken stock
salt and pepper
To complete
2 tablespoons calvados, brandy or cider
2 teaspoons Dijon mustard
4 tablespoons double cream
a small knob butter
225 g (8 oz) eating apple, peeled, cored and sliced
2 teaspoons chopped parsley

Preparation time:	15 minutes plus freezing
Cooking time:	20–22 minutes plus reheating
Microwave setting:	High and conventional hob

—1—

Heat the oil in a frying pan on top of the stove, add the pork and quickly brown all over. Lift out and place on a plate.

—2—

Put the butter and onion in a microwave-proof casserole. Microwave for 3 minutes or until softened, stirring halfway through the cooking time. Stir in the flour, cider, stock and seasoning to taste. Cover and microwave for 2 minutes, stirring after 1 minute.

—3—

Add the pork and any meat juices. Cover and microwave for 10–12 minutes, or until tender.

—4—

Lift out the meat. Cut into thick slices. Put into a rigid freezer container and pour over the sauce. Cool, then freeze for up to three months.

—5—

To use from frozen: Microwave on defrost for about 20 minutes (exact time will depend on microwave and size of container). Microwave on high power for 3–5 minutes until sauce has boiled and pork is piping hot.

—6—

To complete: Remove pork to a warmed serving dish. Add the calvados, brandy or cider, mustard and the cream to the sauce. Microwave on high power for 1 minute. On top of the stove, fry the apple slices in the butter until golden. Add to the sauce. Cover and microwave on high power for 1 minute. Taste for seasoning. Spoon the sauce over the pork and garnish with parsley.

Three-Vegetable Mash

Serves 6
275 g (10 oz) parsnips, peeled and diced
275 g (10 oz) potatoes, peeled and diced
275 g (10 oz) swedes, peeled and diced
75 g (3 oz) unsalted butter or margarine
4–6 tablespoons double cream
salt, pepper and nutmeg to taste

Preparation time:	15 minutes plus freezing
Cooking time:	15 minutes plus reheating
Microwave setting:	High

—1—

Put the parsnips in a large bowl with four tablespoons water. Cover and microwave for 5 minutes.

● It is very important to defrost food slowly and evenly to prevent patches on the food where it has begun to cook. Never try to defrost food quickly by running under a warm or hot tap.

● Food will continue to thaw when removed from the microwave, so allow for "standing time" – defrost whole birds or joints of meat until icy, then leave at normal room temperature to defrost.
● During defrosting, remove giblets from poultry as soon as they loosen, break up any block of fish, mince, sausages or burgers as soon as possible and turn the food regularly.

—2—

Add the prepared potatoes and swedes. Microwave for 10 minutes or until all the vegetables are tender.

—3—

Drain, then roughly mash with the butter and cream until smooth but not quite a purée. Season to taste.

—4—

To freeze: Spoon into a rigid freezer container. Cool, then freeze for up to six months.

—5—

To use from frozen: Thaw on defrost for 25–30 minutes, then reheat on high power for 5 minutes.

Iced Gâteau St Clements

Serves 4 to 6
For the mousse
2 eggs, separated
75 g (3 oz) caster sugar
grated rind and juice of 1 lemon
grated rind and juice of 1 orange
150 ml (¼ pint) double cream, lightly whipped
1 tablespoon orange liqueur (optional)
For the sponge
2 eggs, separated
50 g (2 oz) caster sugar
grated rind and juice of ½ lemon
25 g (1 oz) plain flour
25 g (1 oz) ground almonds
1 tablespoon orange liqueur (optional)
4 tablespoons orange juice
To complete
150 ml (¼ pint) double cream, whipped (optional)
lemon and orange slices
1 × 20 cm (8 in) microwave-proof loaf pan, base-lined

Preparation time:	35 minutes plus freezing
Cooking time:	2½ minutes
Microwave setting:	High

—1—

Whisk the egg yolks with the sugar until very thick, pale and mousse-like (the whisk should leave a ribbon-trail of mixture when lifted). Fold in the lemon and orange rind and juice, followed by the cream and liqueur. Whisk the egg whites until they form soft peaks and fold into the mixture in three batches. Turn the mixture into a freezer container and freeze until firm but not solid – about 1 hour.

—2—

Whisk the egg yolks with the sugar and lemon rind until very thick and pale. Fold in the lemon juice, sifted flour, and ground almonds. Stiffly whisk the egg whites and fold into the mixture in two batches.

—3—

Spoon into the prepared loaf pan and smooth the surface. Microwave for 2½ minutes. Leave the sponge to cool in the loaf pan for 10 minutes then turn out on to a wire rack.

—4—

When completely cold, cut horizontally into three layers. Sprinkle each layer with the liqueur mixed with the orange juice.

—5—

Put the bottom layer of sponge back into the loaf pan. Spoon over half the almost-frozen mousse and even the surface. Open-freeze until firm – about 15 minutes.

—6—

Cover with the middle layer of sponge, and spoon over the remaining mousse. Freeze for 15 minutes, then top with the last layer of sponge. Cover and freeze for up to a month.

—7—

To use from frozen: Trim the sides of the gateau using a sharp knife dipped in hot water. Microwave on defrost for 2 minutes. Decorate with tiny rosettes of cream, and the lemon and orange slices.

Hot Red Pepper Soup

Serves 6

25 g (1 oz) butter or margarine
3 red peppers, weighing about 450 g (1 lb) in total when cored and sliced
1½ tablespoons mild paprika
2 tablespoons flour
900 ml (1½ pints) boiling chicken or turkey stock
a bouquet garni
salt and pepper to taste
To garnish
a few black olives

Preparation time:	15 minutes plus freezing
Cooking time:	18–27 minutes plus reheating
Microwave setting:	High

This bright, spicy soup freezes well, and should be served piping hot for maximum warmth!

—1—

Melt the butter in a large bowl for 1 minute. Stir in peppers and paprika. Cover and microwave for 4–8 minutes until the peppers are tender, stirring halfway through. Stir in the flour, then add the stock and bouquet garni. Cover and microwave for 10–15 minutes.

—2—

Remove the bouquet garni and liquidize or process the soup until smooth. Season well. Reheat for 3 minutes and pour into bowls.

—3—

To garnish: Stone the olives, cut into slivers and sprinkle over the soup.

—4—

To freeze: Freeze without olive garnish in a freezer/microwave-proof container.

—5—

To serve: Defrost in microwave. Reheat on high power for 8–10 minutes until piping hot.

Salmon and Scallop Terrine

Serves 8

12 large spinach leaves – about 175 g (6 oz)
6 small scallops
350 g (12 oz) plaice fillets, skinned
For the salmon mixture
450 g (1 lb) salmon steak
50 g (2 oz) crustless thin sliced white bread
5 tablespoons single cream
1 egg white, lightly beaten
25 g (1 oz) onion, finely chopped
15 g (½ oz) butter
salt, pepper and cayenne
250 ml (8 fl oz) double cream, lightly whipped
1 × 1.5 litre (2½ pint) microwave-proof terrine or loaf pan, base lined

Preparation time:	45 minutes
Cooking time:	20–22 minutes
Microwave setting:	High

—1—

Wash the spinach leaves and remove the stalks. Place the leaves in a polythene bag, fold over the top and microwave on high power for 30–60 seconds. Rinse the leaves with cold water, then pat dry with kitchen paper. Use six of the leaves to line the base and sides of the terrine, leaving the ends to hang over the edge of the terrine.

—2—

Place the scallops in a small bowl, cover with pierced cling film and microwave on high power for 2 minutes. Cool. Wrap each scallop in a spinach leaf. Cut the plaice fillets into long strips 1 cm (½ in) wide.

—3—

Skin the salmon steak and remove the bones. Cut the flesh into thin strips. Place the bread in a bowl and pour over the single cream and egg white. Leave to soak for 5 minutes. Place the onion in a small bowl with the butter. Cover with pierced cling film and microwave on high power for 3 minutes. Leave to cool.

—4—

Mince or process the salmon with the

soaked bread mixture and onion until very smooth. Season well. Put the fish mixture in a basin set over ice and beat in the double cream, a tablespoon at a time.

—5—

Layer the fish in the terrine, starting with a third of the salmon mixture. Arrange half the plaice strips on top, then set the spinach-wrapped scallops down the centre. Cover with another portion of salmon mixture over the top, smooth the surface and cover loosely with cling film. Stand the terrine in a microwave-proof dish half-filled with hot water. Microwave on medium power for 14–16 minutes. (The time will vary according to the shape of the dish.) Remove the terrine, and leave to cool.

To freeze: Double wrap in cling film and freeze.

Chicken Liver Parfait

Serves 6

200 g (7 oz) chicken livers, soaked overnight in milk
100 g (4 oz) butter, melted
3 tablespoons sherry
salt and pepper to taste
6 rashers streaky bacon

To garnish

sprigs of thyme or parsley or wedges of lemon
1 × 600 ml (1 pint) microwave-proof terrine

Preparation time:	20 minutes plus soaking, pressing and freezing
Cooking time:	30 minutes
Microwave setting:	Defrost

A smooth-textured pâté that's quick and simple to prepare and freezes extremely well

—1—

Drain the livers and discard the milk. Place the livers in a blender or processor. Switch on and slowly pour in the melted butter through the hole in the lid. When the mixture is smooth, stir in the sherry and season to taste.

—2—

Stretch the bacon rashers with the back of a knife and use most to line the base and sides of the container. Pour in the liver mixture and place remaining bacon on top.

—3—

Stand in a large non-metallic container half-filled with cold water. Microwave for 30 minutes. Remove from water-bath and allow to cool. Cover with cling film and place weights on top to press the parfait. Leave overnight, remove weights.

—4—

To freeze: Freeze in the container.

—5—

To serve: Microwave on defrost for 11 minutes, wiping away any liquid. Leave to stand 15 minutes. Turn out when completely thawed; serve chilled.

Salmon and Scallop Terrine; Hot Red Pepper Soup

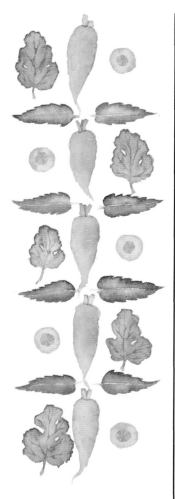

Cream of Carrot and Coriander Soup

Serves 6
1 medium onion, finely chopped
450 g (1 lb) carrots, peeled and sliced
1 clove garlic, crushed
25 g (1 oz) butter or margarine
1 bay leaf
1 tablespoon chopped fresh coriander
300 ml (½ pint) boiling chicken stock
300 ml (½ pint) milk
1 teaspoon sugar
salt and pepper
For the liaison
1 egg yolk
4 tablespoons double cream
To garnish
fresh coriander sprigs

Preparation time:	20 minutes plus freezing
Cooking time:	24–27 minutes plus reheating
Microwave setting:	High

Substitute fresh mint for the coriander if you wish to serve this soup chilled

—1—

Place the onion, carrot and garlic in a bowl with the butter. Cover with cling film and microwave for 6–8 minutes until the carrot is tender. Add the bay leaf, coriander and stock, recover and microwave for 12 minutes. Process or blend until smooth. Return to a clean bowl, add the milk, sugar and seasoning to taste, cover and microwave for 3 minutes.

—2—

For the liaison: Mix together the egg yolk and cream and stir in 2–3 tablespoons of hot soup. Pour into the main soup, stirring well. Microwave for 3–4 minutes.

—3—

Serve garnished with coriander sprigs.

—4—

To freeze: Freeze soup before adding the liaison in a freezer/microwave-proof container.

—5—

To serve: Defrost in microwave, reheat on high power for 10–12 minutes and add liaison as directed above.

Celery and Seafood Pancakes

Serves 4 to 6
8 ready-made pancakes, thawed from frozen
350 g (12 oz) firm fish fillets (haddock, cod or monkfish)
40 g (1½ oz) butter
1 small onion, thinly sliced
3 sticks celery, thinly sliced
3 tablespoons flour
150 ml (¼ pint) milk
150 ml (¼ pint) single cream
2 teaspoons tomato purée
juice of ½ lemon
salt, pepper and cayenne
15 g (½ oz) melted butter
For the sauce aurore
300 ml (½ pint) tinned tomato juice
2 teaspoons arrowroot
100 g (4 oz) shelled prawns
lemon juice to taste
caster sugar
To garnish
whole prawns and celery leaves

Preparation time:	40 minutes plus freezing
Cooking time:	31–37 minutes plus reheating
Microwave setting:	High

—1—

Skin the fish, cut into chunks and place in a buttered dish. Cover with pierced cling film and microwave for 6 minutes. Allow to cool, then flake.

—2—

Place 25 g (1 oz) butter in a jug and microwave for 1 minute. Add the onion and celery and microwave for 2 minutes. Strain, and stir in the flour followed by the milk and cream. Cover and microwave for 6 minutes, whisking every 2 minutes. Stir in the tomato purée, lemon juice and seasoning to taste. Add the flaked fish, onion and celery and allow to cool.

—3—

Divide the filling between the pancakes. Loosely fold the pancakes over the filling and place in a microwave-proof dish. Brush with melted butter, cover with cling film and microwave for 10–12 minutes. Garnish with prawns and celery leaves.

—4—

Place the tomato juice in a jug, cover and microwave for 6–8 minutes until hot.

—5—

Dissolve the arrowroot in one tablespoon cold water and stir into the juice. Microwave for 1–2 minutes, whisking after 1 minute, until thickened. Add prawns, lemon juice, sugar and seasoning to taste. Microwave for 2–3 minutes to heat through.

—6—

To freeze: Open-freeze the filled pancakes, then wrap in a double layer of cling film. *Do not* freeze the sauce.
To serve: Defrost in the microwave. Reheat on high power for 10–12 minutes. Make up the sauce as directed.

Pork and Apricot Casserole

Serves 4
2 tablespoons oil
450 g (1 lb) lean pork, cubed
1 medium onion, finely chopped
1 teaspoon medium curry powder
2 tablespoons flour
300 ml (½ pint) boiling chicken stock
juice and grated rind of 1 large orange
salt and pepper to taste
6 dried apricots, sliced
25 g (1 oz) sultanas
toasted almonds

● Remove all metal ties and clasps before defrosting/ cooking in the microwave.
● When defrosting joints of meat in the microwave, use a thermometer to ensure the meat is totally defrosted all the way through.

Preparation time:	15 minutes plus freezing
Cooking time:	20–25 minutes plus reheating
Microwave setting:	High and conventional hob

A useful winter standby which successfully combines sweet and savoury flavours for a really tasty main course

—1—

Heat 1 tablespoon oil in a large frying pan and quickly brown the pork on all sides.

—2—

Meanwhile place the onion in a large bowl with the remaining oil, cover and microwave for 3 minutes. Stir in the curry powder and flour, then the stock, orange juice and rind. Cover and microwave for 3 minutes.

—3—

Stir well. Add the pork, seasoning, apricots and raisins. Microwave uncovered for 10–15 minutes, stirring halfway through. Taste for seasoning.

—4—

To complete: Scatter with toasted almonds and serve with buttered rice.

—5—

To freeze: Freeze without the toasted almonds in a freezer/microwave-proof container.

—6—

To serve: Defrost in microwave. Reheat on high power for 12–14 minutes. Scatter with toasted almonds and serve.

*Mexican Ratatouille;
Chilled Summer
Soup; Chicken
Cordon Bleu*

Chilled Summer Soup

Serves 6 to 8

1 medium onion, finely chopped
25 g (1 oz) butter
225 g (8 oz) potato, peeled and cubed
450 g (1 lb) minted frozen peas
900 ml (1½ pints) milk
salt, pepper and cayenne to taste
2 tablespoons medium sherry (optional)
150 ml (¼ pint) single cream

To garnish
sprigs of fresh herbs

Preparation time:	15 minutes plus chilling and freezing
Cooking time:	19–22 minutes plus reheating
Microwave setting:	High

This soup retains its lovely delicate colour when prepared in the microwave. Can also be served hot with crusty bread for a good winter warmer

—1—

Place the onion, butter and potato in a large bowl. Cover and microwave for 6–8 minutes. Stir in peas, cover and microwave for 6 minutes, until the potato is tender.

—2—

Add the milk and microwave for 7–8 minutes. Process or liquidize the soup in batches until smooth. Chill.

—3—

Ladle into bowls, swirl in the cream and garnish with herbs.

—4—

To freeze: Freeze in a freezer/microwave-proof container.

—5—

To serve: Defrost in microwave. Reheat for 9–10 minutes until smooth, then chill. Complete with a swirl of cream, garnish and serve.

Chicken Cordon Bleu

Makes 6 servings
12 chicken thighs, boned
6 large slices cooked ham, about 225 g (8 oz)
6 slices Gruyère cheese, about 175 g (6 oz)
6 tablespoons white wine
salt and pepper
50 g (2 oz) button mushrooms, wiped and sliced
To complete
turned mushrooms – see Step 3
watercress

Preparation time:	25 minutes plus freezing
Cooking time:	20–22 minutes plus reheating
Microwave setting:	High and conventional grill

—1—

Trim any fat from the boned chicken thighs and lay out flat on a board. Cut a 6 cm (2½ in) circle from each slice of ham and cheese, using a round pastry cutter. Roughly chop the trimmings, and use to stuff the centres of the thighs. Roll up around the filling and secure the edges with wooden cocktail sticks.

—2—

Place the thighs in a circle in a microwave-proof dish and, pour over the wine. Cover with cling film and microwave for 14–16 minutes until the juices run clear from the chicken. Carefully remove the cocktail sticks and the chicken skins. Cover each piece with a round of ham, then with sliced mushrooms topped by a round of cheese. Place under a hot grill for a few minutes to melt the cheese.

—3—

Turn the mushrooms by removing thin strips of flesh with a canelle knife or sharp paring knife, to give a Catherine-wheel effect. Brush with a little butter and microwave for 2 minutes.

—4—

Arrange the chicken on a serving dish and garnish with turned mushrooms and small bunches of watercress.

—5—

To freeze: Prepare and cook the chicken and grill briefly to just melt the cheese. Cool and open freeze. Wrap individually and label.

—6—

To serve: Defrost in the microwave. Reheat one portion for 4–5 minutes on high power or all six portions for 12–15 minutes. Prepare the turned mushrooms; garnish as above.

Mexican Ratatouille

Serves 4 to 6
450 g (1 lb) courgettes, thinly sliced
1 large onion, thinly sliced
1 green pepper, cored and diced
2 fresh chillies, seeded and finely sliced
450 g (1 lb) tomatoes, skinned and chopped
2 tablespoons olive or vegetable oil
1 clove garlic, crushed
salt and pepper

Preparation time:	15 minutes plus freezing
Cooking time:	10–15 minutes plus reheating
Microwave setting:	High

A good way to use up all those extra vegetables that ripen at the same time. Make in batches for the freezer

—1—

Toss the vegetables in a large bowl with the oil and garlic. Cover with cling film and microwave for 10–15 minutes. Season to taste.

—2—

To freeze: Allow the mixture to cool completely, then freeze in deep rigid containers.

—3—

To serve: Defrost in microwave for 10–12 minutes, stirring occasionally to heat the ratatouille evenly and thoroughly.

Minted Cucumber Soup

Serves 6

1 large cucumber
3 spring onions, trimmed and sliced
900 ml (1½ pints) boiling chicken stock (can be made with stock cubes)
2 teaspoons chopped mint
salt and pepper to taste
1 tablespoon cornflour
4 tablespoons single cream or top milk

To garnish

8 thin slices cucumber
sprigs of fresh mint

Preparation time:	10 minutes plus freezing
Cooking time:	17–22 minutes
Microwave setting:	High

Equally good served hot or cold

—1—

Cut 8 thin slices of cucumber, wrap in cling film and keep aside.

—2—

Chop the cucumber and mix with the spring onions. Put into a large microwave-proof bowl and pour over the boiling stock. Cover and microwave for 12–15 minutes. Stir in the mint and season to taste. Liquidize the soup.

—3—

Mix the cornflour with the cream or top milk, stir into the soup and microwave for 3–5 minutes to thicken, stirring frequently to prevent lumps forming.

—4—

Serve piping hot or allow to cool and chill before serving garnished with cucumber slices and mint sprigs.

—5—

To freeze: Allow soup to cool completely before freezing in a freezer/microwave-proof container.

—6—

To thaw: Microwave on defrost for 20–30 minutes, stirring occasionally, or thaw at room temperature for about 5 hours. Re-season if necessary before serving. To serve cold, garnish with cucumber slices and mint sprigs. To serve hot, after defrosting microwave on high power for 7–8 minutes.

Navarin of Lamb with Onion Dumplings

Serves 4 to 6

1 kg (2 lb) lean lamb
2 tablespoons soya oil
1 teaspoon brown sugar
1 tablespoon flour
600 ml (1 pint) lamb or chicken stock
2 tablespoons tomato purée
salt and pepper to taste
a bouquet garni
4 small onions, peeled
2 carrots, peeled
1 small turnip, peeled

For the dumplings

75 g (3 oz) self-raising flour
½ teaspoon salt
2 spring onions, chopped
40 g (1½ oz) shredded suet

Preparation time:	40 minutes plus freezing
Cooking time:	47–48 minutes
Microwave setting:	High

We discovered the meat was particularly tender if cooked the day before, then reheated when you make the dumplings

—1—

Cut the meat into 2.5 cm (1 in) cubes. Put the oil into a shallow microwave-proof casserole and microwave for 30–60 seconds. Add the meat, cover with cling film and microwave for 16 minutes, stirring occasionally. Remove the meat and reserve.

—2—

Discard all but two tablespoons of the fat. Stir the sugar and flour into the fat, and microwave for 30 seconds. Stir in the stock and microwave until the mixture boils (about 1 minute). Add the tomato purée, seasoning and bouquet garni. Microwave for 2–3 minutes.

—3—

Quarter the onions, cut the carrots and turnip into match sticks. Add to the casserole with the meat. Cover with lid or cling film and microwave for 20 minutes. (Leave to cool at this point if you wish to serve the next day. Then reheat before adding the dumplings.)

—4—

Prepare the dumplings by mixing all the ingredients together with enough cold water to make a soft but not sticky dough. Roll the mixture into 12 balls. Carefully add to the casserole, cover and microwave for 7 minutes. Taste for seasoning before serving.

—5—

To freeze: Freeze before adding the dumplings.

—6—

To serve: Defrost in microwave. Prepare the dumplings as directed. Microwave the navarin on high power for 12–15 minutes, adding the dumplings after 3 minutes.

● The time taken to defrost or reheat will depend on the shape, size and density of the food as well as the shape and size of the dish, and according to the power setting of the microwave.
● Defrost cakes, bread and pastry dishes on kitchen paper towels to absorb any excess moisture.
● Don't defrost cream, egg whites, meringues, or iced cakes in the microwave.

Lemon Cheese

Serves 4 to 6
300 ml (½ pint) double cream
150 ml (¼ pint) soured cream or Greek yogurt
3 tablespoons caster sugar
grated rind and juice of 2 large lemons
1 sachet powdered gelatine

Preparation time:	15 minutes plus freezing
Cooking time:	1–2 minutes
Microwave setting:	High

A rich, creamy lemon dessert to serve with fresh fruit – particularly raspberries

—1—

Whip the double cream until thick and light. Carefully fold in the soured cream or yogurt and the sugar, the grated rind of 1 lemon and the juice of both lemons.

—2—

Sprinkle the gelatine over 3 tablespoons water in a small bowl or cup. Leave to soak for a couple of minutes then microwave for 1–2 minutes, then gently stir it into the lemon mixture.

—3—

Spoon into a bowl or mould. Decorate with remaining grated rind, cover and freeze.

—4—

To serve: To eat frozen, microwave on defrost for 45 seconds until soft enough to scoop. To eat as a mousse microwave on defrost for 3–4 minutes, then leave to stand until completely thawed.

From the top:
Chocolate Almond
Bombe (p 146); The
Chocolate Cake
(p 148); White
Chocolate Mousse
(p 147); Rich
Chocolate Shortcake
(p 147); Chocolate
Truffles (p 150);
Orange and
Chocolate Straws
(p 151); Hazelnut
Ganache Chocolates
(p 151)

Tempting treats

PUDDINGS & DESSERTS

Wonderful puddings and light, delicious desserts make any meal complete. Many of these recipes make good use of fruit — fresh and frozen — bringing seasonal and year-round pleasure to the table. The microwave is ideal for poaching fruit and making purées; it also makes wonderfully light sponge puddings. And of course no collection of desserts would be complete without some treats for the chocaholics in our midst. Our wonderful array of chocolate treats — truffles, chocolate ganache, mousse, and of course the obligatory chocolate cake — should satisfy the cravings of the most desperate addict.

Chocolate Almond Bombe

Serves 8 to 10
For the sponge
1 egg
25 g (1 oz) caster sugar
1 tablespoon cocoa
20 g (¾ oz) plain flour
2 tablespoons Amaretto liqueur
For the dark chocolate parfait
40 g (1½ oz) caster sugar
100 g (4 oz) plain chocolate
2 egg yolks
210 ml (7½ fl oz) double cream, whipped
For the white chocolate parfait
50 g (2 oz) caster sugar
175 g (6 oz) white chocolate
3 egg yolks
300 ml (½ pint) double cream, whipped
75 g (3 oz) blanched almonds, toasted and
chopped
To complete
50 g (2 oz) toasted slivered almonds
1 × 15 cm (6 in) soufflé dish, greased and base-
lined
1 × 1.2 litre (2 pint) freezer-proof bowl

Preparation time:	30 minutes plus freezing
Cooking time:	8½–10½ minutes
Microwave setting:	Low and High

An elegant, frozen pudding of dark chocolate parfait over chocolate sponge, and a
white chocolate parfait in the centre

—1—

For the sponge: Whisk the egg with the
sugar until very thick and light – the whisk,
when lifted, should leave a ribbon-trail of
mixture.

—2—

Mix the cocoa with one tablespoon warm
water to a smooth paste in a cup or small
bowl. Cover and microwave on low power
for 30 seconds.

—3—

Sieve the flour and carefully fold into the
egg mixture with the cocoa paste. Spoon
into the prepared soufflé dish and spread
evenly. Microwave on high power for 4–5
minutes until just set. Cool, then sprinkle
with the liqueur.

—4—

For the dark chocolate parfait: Put the
sugar into a bowl with three tablespoons of
water and microwave on high power for 1
minute or until dissolved. Stir, then microwave on high power for 1–2 minutes, to
thoroughly boil.

—5—

Chop the chocolate and carefully blend into
the sugar syrup. Work in the egg yolks one
at a time. Cool, then fold in the whipped
cream. Place the mixture in the freezer for
20–30 minutes or until the mixture is *half-*
frozen. Spread this mixture evenly over the
base and sides of the freezer-proof bowl.
Freeze until solid.

—6—

For the white chocolate parfait: Make as
above but dissolve the sugar in *four* tablespoons water. Pour into container, freeze
for 1 hour, then fold in almonds.

—7—

To assemble: Cut the sponge into several
pieces and use to neatly line the chocolate
mixture in the bowl. Return the bowl to the
freezer until the sponge is firm. Spoon the
white chocolate mixture into the centre.
Cover and freeze for up to three months.

—8—

To serve: Microwave on low power for 2
minutes, turn out on to a serving plate and
scatter the almonds over the top.

White Chocolate Mousse

Serves 6
2 egg yolks
2 tablespoons caster sugar
4 tablespoons dry vermouth
100 g (4 oz) white chocolate, chopped
300 ml (½ pint) whipping cream
chocolate shapes or grated chocolate to decorate
a large freezer-proof serving dish or six
individual dishes

Preparation time: 10 minutes plus
chilling or freezing
Cooking time: 2 minutes
Microwave setting: High

Use a good quality white chocolate for this delicious dinner-party dessert

—*1*—

Put the egg yolks, sugar and half the vermouth in a bowl. Whisk with a mixer (electric or rotary) until very thick and mousse-like.

—*2*—

Put the chocolate and remaining vermouth into a small bowl and microwave for 2 minutes, stirring after 1 minute.

—*3*—

Whip the cream until it just forms soft peaks.

—*4*—

Fold the yolk mixture into the chocolate, followed by the cream. Spoon into the dish or dishes and cover. Freeze for up to a month (or chill overnight in the fridge).

—*5*—

To use from frozen: Microwave on defrost for 2 minutes, then decorate with chocolate leaves and eat while still semi-frozen.

Rich Chocolate Shortcake

Makes one 20 cm (8 in) round
175 g (6 oz) plain flour
25 g (1 oz) rice flour
25 g (1 oz) cocoa
a pinch of salt
150 g (5 oz) unsalted butter
50 g (2 oz) caster sugar
icing sugar to sprinkle
a large flat plate or microwave turntable base
lined with cling film

Preparation time: 10 minutes plus
cooling
Cooking time: 4½ minutes
Microwave setting: High

Delicious by itself or topped with fresh fruit and cream for a delightful dessert

—*1*—

Sift the flours with the cocoa and salt. Dice the butter and rub in, using the tips of your fingers. Stir in the sugar. Knead lightly to form a ball of dough. Press out on the plate to form a 20 cm (8 in) round of even thickness. Pinch the edges to decorate.

—*2*—

Microwave for 4½ minutes, checking frequently, until firm.

—*3*—

Cool. Lift off the plate.

—*4*—

To freeze: Mark into eight sections and open-freeze. Wrap and store for up to three months.

—*5*—

To use from frozen: Thaw on defrost for 5–10 minutes, then stand on a wire rack for 15 minutes. Sprinkle with icing sugar before serving.

The Chocolate Cake

Makes one 20 cm (8 in) cake
For the cake
100 g (4 oz) softened butter
175 g (6 oz) caster sugar
2 egg yolks
150 g (5 oz) plain flour
3 teaspoons baking powder
50 ml (2 fl oz) soya oil
50 g (2 oz) cocoa
3 egg whites
For the filling and topping
150 ml (¼ pint) double cream
175 g (6 oz) plain chocolate, chopped
1 × 20 cm (8 in) microwave-proof deep dish or
soufflé case, base-lined

Preparation time:	15 minutes plus cooling and freezing, if desired
Cooking time:	8½ minutes plus standing
Microwave setting:	High

A light and fluffy cake mixture filled and topped with a rich chocolate ganâche mixture, which can be made in advance and frozen

—1—

Cream the butter and sugar until light and fluffy. Beat in the egg yolks, one at a time. Sift the flour with the baking powder, and gently fold in alternately with the oil.

—2—

In a cup, mix the cocoa to a paste with six tablespoons boiling water. Microwave for 30 seconds. Stir into the cake mixture, and blend thoroughly. Whisk the egg whites until firm but not stiff, and fold into the mixture. Spoon into the dish.

—3—

Microwave for 6 minutes. Leave to stand for 10 minutes, then turn out on to a wire rack and cool.

—4—

To freeze: The chocolate sponge can be open-frozen at this point. Open-freeze until solid, then wrap well and label. Store for up to three months.

—5—

To use from frozen: Thaw the chocolate sponge on de-frost for 15 minutes. Leave to stand for 1 hour until thawed. Slice the cake into four horizontal layers.

—6—

To make the filling and topping: Microwave the cream for 2 minutes. Pour on to the chocolate and stir until smooth. Leave to cool, stirring frequently.

—7—

Beat rapidly for a minute until the mixture thickens, then use half to sandwich the cake. Spread the remaining mixture over the top and sides. Leave until set.

Variation
The cake can be frozen complete with the filling and topping, provided the base has not been previously frozen. The filled cake is best left to thaw at room temperature overnight.

Pommes Bristol

Serves 6
3 medium oranges, washed
6 even-sized dessert apples
175 g (6 oz) granulated sugar
For the caramel chips
50 g (2 oz) caster sugar

Preparation time:	20 minutes plus cooling and setting
Cooking time:	23–25 minutes
Microwave setting:	High

A classic French dessert that is quickly and easily prepared in the microwave

● To soften marzipan before moulding microwave on high for 10 to 15 seconds.
● To flambé spirits, heat the spirit in a tough microwave-proof bowl for 20 seconds on high.

Left: Pommes Bristol; Below: Tipsy Pears (p 150)

—1—

Using a vegetable peeler, remove the outer skin of the oranges, avoiding the pith, and cut into thin needle-like shreds. Place in a bowl with 85 ml (3 fl oz) water. Cover and microwave for 3–4 minutes until boiling. Drain and set the shreds aside.

—2—

Place the granulated sugar in a large bowl with 300 ml (½ pint) water. Microwave for 4 minutes, stirring every minute, until the sugar dissolves. Peel and carefully core the apples. Slide into the syrup. Cover and microwave for 10 minutes until the apples are tender. Cool.

—3—

Peel the pared oranges with a sharp knife to remove the pith, then cut into segments. Place the cooled apples in a serving dish and top with the orange segments. Stir the orange-skin shreds into the syrup and pour over the apples.

—4—

For the caramel chips. Place the caster sugar in a bowl with three tablespoons water. Microwave until a good caramel colour – about 6–7 minutes. Pour on to an oiled baking sheet and leave to set. Crush into chips with a rolling pin. (The chips can be stored in an airtight container for up to a week.)

—5—

Scatter caramel chips over the apples and serve with fresh cream or yogurt.

Tipsy Pears

Serves 4
4 even-sized ripe pears
150 ml (¼ pint) red wine
100 g (4 oz) demerara sugar
6 tablespoons crème de cassis
2 tablespoons toasted flaked almonds

Preparation time:	10 minutes plus chilling
Cooking time:	26–32 minutes
Microwave setting:	High

The microwaving time for the pears will vary according to their size and ripeness, so check to ensure that they are completely cooked

—1—

Find a deep dish into which the pears fit snugly. Put the wine, 150 ml (¼ pint) water and sugar into the dish and microwave for 12 minutes, stirring halfway through.

—2—

Peel the pears, leaving the stalks on. Turn the pears upside down and carefully core from underneath.

—3—

Slide the pears into the syrup and microwave for 2–5 minutes. Add one tablespoon of the cassis and gently move the pears in the syrup. Microwave for 3–4 minutes until the pears are tender.

—4—

Carefully lift the pears out of the syrup using a slotted spoon (not by the stalks as they will come off) and put them in a serving dish.

—5—

Return the syrup to the oven and microwave for 9–11 minutes or until syrupy. Stir in the remaining cassis. Pour over the pears and leave to cool. Chill. Scatter the flaked almonds over the pear and serve with whipped cream.

Chocolate Truffles

Makes 12
75 g (3 oz) plain chocolate
1 egg yolk
15 g (½ oz) butter
1 teaspoon single cream
1 teaspoon rum or brandy
25 g (1 oz) Amaretti (macaroon) biscuits, finely crushed
To coat
1 tablespoon each icing sugar and cocoa powder

Preparation time:	10 minutes plus chilling
Cooking time:	2 minutes
Microwave setting:	High

Rich and luxurious for a special treat

—1—

Break up the chocolate and place in a small bowl. Microwave for 2 minutes or until melted.

—2—

Stir in the remaining ingredients and beat the mixture until it thickens. Chill until firm enough to handle.

—3—

Shape the mixture into 12 balls. Put the icing sugar and cocoa into a small plastic bag. Shake until mixed, then toss the truffles in the mixture to coat evenly.

—4—

Chill until firm then store in a cool, dry place.

Orange and Chocolate Straws

Makes 18 to 24
For the pastry
100 g (4 oz) plain flour
25 g (1 oz) cocoa powder
grated rind of 1 orange
100 g (4 oz) unsalted butter, chilled
beaten egg to glaze
caster sugar to sprinkle
To complete
100 g (4 oz) white chocolate
100 g (4 oz) dark chocolate

Preparation time:	40 minutes plus chilling
Cooking time:	14–18 minutes
Microwave setting:	High and conventional oven

Pretty and elegant, these edible 'decorations' for a festive table are irresistible!

—1—

For the pastry: Sift the flour and cocoa into a mixing bowl and add the finely-diced butter and orange rind. Mix quickly to coat the fat with the flour. Stir in six tablespoons cold water to make a soft but not too sticky, lumpy-looking dough.

—2—

Turn on to a floured work surface and form into a brick shape. Roll out to an oblong 1 cm (½ in) thick, then fold into three like an envelope. Give the dough a quarter turn and repeat until the pastry has had four rolls and folds. Wrap and chill for 30 minutes.

—3—

Roll the pastry out to a 20 cm (8 in) square about 5 mm (¼) thick. Brush with beaten egg and sprinkle with caster sugar. Roll again until the pastry is 3 mm (⅛ in) thick. Cut into strips 10 by 1 cm (4 by ½ in). Twist once to form "straws", place on greased baking sheets and chill for 20 minutes.

—4—

Bake in a conventional oven set at Gas Mark 7, 425 degrees F, 220 degrees C, for 12–15 minutes until crisp. Cool on wire racks.

—5—

To complete: Put the white chocolate into a small bowl. Microwave for 2–3 minutes until melted and stir until smooth.

—6—

Dip one end of each straw in the white chocolate and scrape off the excess. Leave to set on waxed paper. Melt the dark chocolate as for the white and dip the other ends. Leave to set. Store in an airtight container.

Hazelnut Ganache Chocolates

Makes 30 to 34
100 ml (3½ fl oz) double cream
200 g (7 oz) dark chocolate, chopped
90 g (3½ oz) chopped toasted hazelnuts
1½ tablespoons Grand Marnier
foil sweet cases

Preparation time:	10 minutes plus chilling
Cooking time:	2–3 minutes
Microwave setting:	High

—1—

Place the cream in a jug and microwave for 2–3 minutes until scalding hot. Stir in the chocolate and leave to melt. Stir until smooth.

—2—

Leave to cool then beat well with an electric beater until very light and thick. Fold in the nuts and liqueur.

—3—

Spoon carefully into the sweet cases and chill until firm.

Damson and Orange Pancakes

Serves 4 to 6

8 ready-made pancakes, thawed if frozen
450 g (1 lb) damsons, washed
2 oranges
150 g (5 oz) caster sugar
25 g (1 oz) chopped walnuts
2 tablespoons Cointreau or orange juice

Preparation time:	15 minutes plus standing
Cooking time:	10–13 minutes
Microwave setting:	High

Keep ready-cooked pancakes in the freezer and thaw in your microwave for a speedy dessert. If damsons are unavailable, ripe peaches make a delicious substitute

—*1*—

Stone the damsons and place in a bowl with the grated rind and juice of one orange and 100 g (4 oz) sugar. Cover and micro-wave for 8–10 minutes or until tender.

—*2*—

Peel the other orange and carefully cut out the segments, discarding any pips and pith. Stir the orange segments into the damsons with the chopped walnuts and leave to stand for 5 minutes.

—*3*—

Spoon the filling into the pancakes and roll up or fold into quarters. Place on a serving dish. Stir the remaining sugar into the Cointreau and spoon over the pancakes. Microwave for 2–3 minutes to reheat.

—*4*—

Serve with whipped cream – spiked with Cointreau, if you dare!

Cranachan

Serves 6
50 g (2 oz) medium oatmeal
300 ml (½ pint) whipping cream
2 tablespoons clear honey
3 tablespoons whisky
225 g (8 oz) raspberries

Preparation time:	5 minutes plus cooling
Cooking time:	7–8 minutes
Microwave setting:	High

A rich and creamy dessert in the true Scottish tradition. If using frozen cream, defrost it in the microwave for a couple of minutes but be sure to chill it again before whipping or it will not hold its shape

—1—

Spread the oatmeal evenly on a large plate and microwave for 7–8 minutes, stirring frequently, until golden. Cool completely.

—2—

Whip the cream until it forms soft peaks, then gradually whisk in the honey and whisky. Gently fold through the oatmeal.

—3—

Divide the raspberries between six long-stemmed glasses and top with the oatmeal cream. Serve at room temperature accompanied by almond biscuits.

Plum Fool

175 g (6 oz) ripe plums
1–2 tablespoons demerara sugar
large pinch mixed spice
2 tablespoons thick set natural yogurt
2 tablespoons double cream, lightly whipped
a drop of almond essence

Preparation time:	10 minutes plus chilling
Cooking time:	4–5 minutes
Microwave setting:	High

Serve chilled with crisp almond biscuits

—1—

Wash, halve and stone the plums. Put into a bowl with the sugar, spice and one tablespoon water. Cover and microwave for 4–5 minutes until tender.

—2—

Sieve to make a smooth purée. Cool.

—3—

Mix the yogurt and cream with a drop of almond essence. Swirl through the plum purée to give a marbled effect. Chill for several hours before serving.

Plum Crumble Pie

Makes one 20 cm (8 in) pie
450 g (1 lb) plums, stoned and sliced
1 × 20 cm (8 in) pre-baked wholemeal flan case
1 tablespoon honey
For the topping
50 g (2 oz) butter or margarine
100 g (4 oz) jumbo rolled oats
40 g (1½ oz) brown sugar
2 teaspoons ground mixed spice

Preparation time:	5 minutes
Cooking time:	7 minutes 45 seconds
Microwave setting:	High

Pastry is better cooked in a conventional oven rather than a microwave, so we have used a ready-baked flan case.

—1—

Arrange the plums in the flan case and drizzle over the honey.

—2—

Put the butter in a small bowl and microwave for 45 seconds.

—3—

Stir in the oats, sugar and spice. Mix well, then spoon on top of the plums. Microwave for 7 minutes. Serve hot or warm with ice cream.

Hot Cranberry Compôte with Cinnamon Dumplings

Serves 4 to 6
225 g (8 oz) cranberries, fresh or frozen
100 g (4 oz) raspberries, fresh or frozen
350 g (12 oz) cooking apples
50 g (2 oz) caster sugar, or to taste
For the dumplings
50 g (2 oz) self-raising flour
25 g (1 oz) butter or margarine
2 teaspoons caster sugar
a large pinch of cinnamon
2 tablespoons milk
2 tablespoons demerara sugar
1 × 1.5 litre (2½ pint) shallow microwave-proof dish

Preparation time:	15 minutes
Cooking time:	12–13 minutes
Microwave setting:	Defrost, then High

Tiny spiced dumplings make a lovely contrast to the slightly tart fruit in this delicious and unusual pudding

—1—

If using frozen fruit, thaw on defrost in the microwave.

—2—

Peel, core and slice the cooking apples and put in the dish with the cranberries and four tablespoons water. Cover and microwave on high power for 6 minutes, stirring halfway through.

—3—

Add the raspberries and sugar. Stir well, cover and microwave on high power for 4–5 minutes or until the fruit is soft but not pulpy. Allow to stand while making the dumplings.

—4—

Sift the flour into a bowl and rub in the fat. Stir in the sugar and cinnamon. Bind to a soft but not sticky dough with the milk. Roll the dough into small balls and drop into the fruit. Cover and microwave on high power for 2 minutes until the dumplings have puffed up and are cooked through. Sprinkle over the demerara sugar and serve with whipped cream or thick-set yogurt.

French Prune Tart

Serves 4 to 6
For the base
100 g (4 oz) digestive biscuits, crushed
25 g (1 oz) demerara sugar
50 g (2 oz) butter or margarine
For the filling
100 g (4 oz) stoned, ready-to-eat prunes
65 ml (2½ fl oz) double or whipping cream
2 eggs, beaten
50 g (2 oz) caster sugar
a few drops of vanilla essence
40 g (1½ oz) ground almonds
2 tablespoons orange flower
water (optional)
1 tablespoon brandy
1 × 20 cm (8 in) microwave-proof shallow flan dish

Preparation time:	15 minutes
Cooking time:	11½ minutes plus standing
Microwave setting:	High

A sweet and luxurious way to eat prunes. Serve warm or at room temperature, accompanied by cream or ice cream

—1—

To make the base: mix the biscuits with the sugar. Melt the butter in the microwave for 1½ minutes. Stir into the biscuit mixture.

When well mixed, press evenly over the base and sides of the flan dish.

—2—

For the filling: roughly chop the prunes and scatter over the biscuit base. Whisk together all the remaining ingredients and pour into the flan case.

—3—

Microwave for 10 minutes or until set. Leave the tart to stand for 5 minutes, then sprinkle over the brandy.

Three Fruit Terrine

Serves 6 to 8
300 ml (½ pint) milk
3 egg yolks
85 g (3 oz) caster sugar
a few drops vanilla essence
2 tablespoons Grand Marnier (optional)
15 g (½ oz) gelatine powder
200 ml (7 fl oz) double cream
175 g (6 oz) loganberries or raspberries
175 g (6 oz) blackberries
2 small ripe peaches
1 × 1.2 litre (2 pint) terrine, base-lined

Preparation time:	25 minutes plus cooling and chilling
Cooking time:	7 minutes
Microwave setting:	High

This elegant fruit terrine would make a lovely finish to a late summer dinner party

—1—

Put the milk in a jug and microwave for 3 minutes until just boiling. Whisk the egg yolks and sugar together in a jug and pour on the milk, whisking continuously.

—2—

Return to the microwave and microwave for 2–3 minutes, whisking every minute, until the custard thickens. Take care not to let it curdle. Stir in the vanilla essence and Grand Marnier, if using, and leave to cool.

—3—

Sprinkle the gelatine over three tablespoons cold water in a small bowl. Leave to soak for 5 minutes. Microwave for 40–60 seconds until melted. Cool slightly then stir into the cooled custard. Whip the double cream until it forms soft peaks. Fold into the custard, and chill until almost set.

—4—

When ready to assemble the terrine, wash the loganberries and blackberries. Pour boiling water over the peaches and leave to stand for 30 seconds. Drain, then run under cold water. Peel off the skins, halve the peaches and remove the stones. Thinly slice the flesh.

—5—

Beat the nearly-set custard well until thick and smooth. Spread one third in the base of the terrine and cover with half the prepared fruit. Spoon over half the remaining custard, then the rest of the fruit. Finish with the remaining custard and smooth the surface. Chill until set.

—6—

Turn out on to a plate and cut in thick slices. Serve with pouring cream or a quick sauce made from puréed raspberries sweetened to taste.

● When making jams and marmalades, warm the bag of sugar in the microwave – it will dissolve at a faster rate when added to the fruit.
● If making jams or marmalade in the microwave, remember not to leave the thermometer in the bowl while the microwave is switched on. The fruit and sugar will bubble up a lot during cooking, so to prevent spillages and burning, use a large bowl and don't be tempted to overfill. Wear oven gloves when removing the bowl to reduce the risk of burns.
● Jars and bottles can be sterilised in the microwave ready for preserving. Just fill clean jars one-third full with water, and microwave on 'high' for 2 to 3 minutes. Lift out carefully then drain and dry.
● Citrus fruit can be microwaved on high for 1 to 2 minutes before squeezing, to extract more juice.

Useful Hints on Meat Cookery

GUIDE TO DEFROSTING MEAT – JOINTS

Meat	Time per 450 g (1 lb) on Defrost power	Total standing time	Special points
Beef, boned & rolled	7–8 minutes	60 minutes	Turn over and on sides during defrosting.
Beef, joints on bone	9–10 minutes	60 minutes	Cover bone end with foil during defrosting and turn over.
Lamb, leg	8–9 minutes	15–20 minutes	Cover knuckle end of joint with foil halfway through defrosting and turn over.
Lamb, shoulder	6–7 minutes	15–20 minutes	Foreleg may need covering with foil during defrosting. Turn over.
Pork, top fillet of leg.	7–8 minutes	60 minutes	Turn over during defrosting.
Veal, leg	7–8 minutes	15–20 minutes	Cover knuckle end of joint halfway through defrosting. Turn over.
Veal, shoulder	6–7 minutes	15–20 minutes	If any foreleg, cover with foil halfway through defrosting and turn over.

GUIDE TO DEFROSTING MEAT – SMALLER CUTS

Type and weight of meat	Time on Defrost power	Standing time	Special points
Bacon 225 g (8 oz)	3–4 minutes	5 minutes	Separate rashers during defrosting.
Cubed meat Stewing/Braising 450 g (1 lb)	8–9 minutes	8–10 minutes	Separate pieces of meat during defrosting.
Kidneys 450 g (1 lb)	4–5 minutes		Separate kidneys and leave to defrost naturally.
Lamb chops 2 × 100 g (4 oz)	4–5 minutes	5–6 minutes	Separate chops during defrosting.
Liver 450 g (1 lb)	4–5 minutes		Separate slices and leave to defrost naturally.
Minced meat 450 g (1 lb)	8–9 minutes	8–10 minutes	Break up with a fork twice during defrosting. Remove any thawed meat.
Sausages 450 g (1 lb)	5–6 minutes	8–10 minutes	Separate and rearrange halfway through defrosting.
Steak Individual thick	3–4 minutes		Leave to defrost naturally.
Individual thin	2–3 minutes		Leave to defrost naturally.

■ The most successfully cooked joints are of an even shape and free from bone. They should be lean with an even marbling of fat and a thin outer layer of fat.

■ If a joint does contain bone and is of an uneven shape, for example a leg of lamb, the thinner end should be shielded with aluminium foil for at least half of the cooking time to prevent it from drying and toughening the texture of the meat.

■ A degree of browning does occur, particularly with the larger cuts of meat which are cooked over a longer period.

■ Pork rind should be scored and salt rubbed in to crisp the surface. If any part of the skin remains soft after cooking, just cut it off in strips and briefly heat in the microwave cooker; they will soon crackle.

■ All meats will spatter a little during cooking, but a loose cover contains such particles around the meat.

■ Meat should preferably be raised above its own juices when cooking, for which a microwave roasting rack can be used. Alternatively the meat can be placed on an inverted saucer or plate in a shallow dish and loosely covered with greaseproof paper or a slit roasting bag. As fat and juices accumulate, remove them and set aside to make the gravy to serve with the meat.

■ Meat can also be cooked in a roasting bag with the ends loosely secured with string or with a strip from the end of the bag. Pierce the bag to allow some of the steam to escape and place the meat in a shallow dish for cooking.

■ It is essential that all meats are allowed a standing period of 15–20 minutes depending on the density of the joint. After cooking, remove the meat from the oven and cover with a foil tent. During the first 5–6 minutes the internal temperature will increase several degrees.

■ If using a microwave thermometer the following is a guide to temperatures. They are based on the internal temperature of the meat on completion of cooking.

Meat	INTERNAL TEMPERATURE ON REMOVAL FROM OVEN	
BEEF (rare)	56°C	133°F
BEEF (medium)	65°C	150°F
BEEF (well done)	70°C	160°F
LAMB	76°C	168°F
VEAL	76°C	168°F
PORK	80°C	175°F
GAMMON	65°C	150°F

Useful Hints on Vegetable Cooking

GUIDE TO FROZEN VEGETABLE COOKING			
Vegetable	**Quantity**	**Container/Method**	**Cooking time**
Asparagus	225 g (8 oz)	Covered shallow dish. Add 2 tablespoons water.	6–7 minutes + 3 minutes standing
Beans Broad French Runner	225 g (8 oz) 225 g (8 oz) 225 g (8 oz)	Covered shallow dish. Add 2 tablespoons water. Covered shallow dish. Add 2 tablespoons water. Covered shallow dish. Add 3 tablespoons water.	7–8 minutes + 3 minutes standing 6–7 minutes + 2 minutes standing 5–6 minutes + 2 minutes standing
Broccoli	225 g (8 oz)	Covered shallow dish. Add 2 tablespoons water.	6–7 minutes + 2 minutes standing
Brussels sprouts	225 g (8 oz)	Covered shallow dish. Add 4 tablespoons water.	7–8 minutes + 3 minutes standing
Cauliflower florets	225 g (8 oz)	Covered shallow dish. Add 4 tablespoons water.	6–7 minutes + 3 minutes standing
Carrots	225 g (8 oz) whole	Covered shallow dish. Add 2 tablespoons water.	6–7 minutes + 3 minutes standing
Corn-on-the-cob	2 ears	Wrap in buttered greaseproof paper.	6–7 minutes + 2 minutes standing
Courgettes	225 g (8 oz)	Covered shallow dish. Add 2 tablespoons water.	4–5 minutes + 2 minutes standing
Leaf spinach	225 g (8 oz)	Covered shallow dish.	5–6 minutes + 2 minutes standing
Mixed vegetables	225 g (8 oz)	Cook in pouch and pierce top. Flex pouch during cooking.	5–6 minutes + 2 minutes standing
Onions, sliced	225 g (8 oz)	Covered shallow dish.	3–4 minutes
Peas	225 g (8 oz)	Cook in pouch and pierce top. Flex pouch during cooking.	4–5 minutes + 2 minutes standing
Stewpack	225 g (8 oz)	Cook in pouch and pierce top. Flex pouch during cooking.	6–7 minutes + 2 minutes standing
Sweetcorn	225 g (8 oz)	Cook in pouch and pierce top. Flex pouch during cooking.	4–5 minutes +2 minutes standing

■ Courgettes and leeks, once trimmed and sliced, need rinsing and draining, but the water adhering to the vegetables is sufficient for cooking. The same principle applies to fresh spinach.

■ Most other vegetables require 2–4 tablespoons of water for cooking.

■ Boiling bags and roasting bags are easy for vegetable cookery, but do not use metal ties on the bag.

■ Seasoning can be added to the water for cooking but not too much, for the fresh natural flavour requires little addition.

■ Seasoning and a knob of butter can be added after cooking if preferred.

■ Stir or rearrange the vegetables during the cooking cycle.

■ Cook new potatoes in their skins, with a little salted water added to the dish.

Useful Hints on Cooking Fish

■ If cooking several at once, arrange the fish fillets with the tails overlapping and towards the centre of the dish.

■ Allow fish to stand for approximately 3–4 minutes after cooking. It will retain its heat and give you time to make any accompanying sauces.

■ 'Boil in the Bag' fish should have the pouch pierced before heating.

■ Cook all fish on Maximum (Full) power, unless manufacturers recommend otherwise.

■ Recipes involving fish in batter are not successful for microwave cooking, as you must not attempt to deep fat fry (see page 37 for further details).

GUIDE TO DEFROSTING AND COOKING FISH			
Fish	**Quantity**	**Time on Defrost power**	**Standing time**
Crabmeat	225 g (8 oz)	6–7 minutes	5 minutes
Fish fillets, Cod, Plaice, Haddock, etc.	450 g (1 lb)	7–8 minutes	5 minutes
Fish steak	175 g (6 oz)	2–3 minutes	3 minutes
Fish steaks	2 × 175 g (6 oz)	4–5 minutes	5 minutes
Mackerel	2 × 350 g (12 oz)	10–12 minutes	8 minutes
Prawns, Scampi	100 g (4 oz) 450 g (1 lb)	2–2½ minutes 6–7 minutes	3 minutes 5 minutes
Scallops	450 g (1 lb)	8–9 minutes	5 minutes
Trout, Herring	1 × 1¼ kg (3 lb)	15–16 minutes	10 minutes
Whole fish, gutted	2 × 225 g (8 oz)	8–9 minutes	8 minutes

INDEX

ACKNOWLEDGEMENTS

Microwave courtesy of Brother Industries.
Front cover photograph by Ian O'Leary.
Illustrations By Nadine Wickenden.

VOLTAGE VARIATIONS

All the microwave ovens used while devising and testing these recipes ranged between 600 and 700 watts in output. So for these recipes, food to be cooked on 'high' means on full power, or the maximum setting for the microwave of 600–700 watts.

Timings will alter if your microwave has a different output.

If 'high', or full power, on your particular oven is 400–450 watts, then increase the cooking time by about a third; if it is 500–550 watts on your oven, increase the cooking time by about one fifth. (Use the 'high' setting for cooking fish, chicken, bacon, drinks and vegetables.)

Cooking on 'medium' means using 60 per cent of the full power of your microwave (use this setting for casseroles) and food cooked on 'low' means using about 35 per cent of full power (use 'low' for melting butter, gelatine and chocolate, also for cooking egg and cheese dishes).

PVC clingfilm
On 22nd July 1986 the Ministry of Agriculture issued a warning concerning the use of PVC clingfilm for cooking, and as many of the recipes in this book refer to the use of this material we feel it right to draw this to our readers' attention. There is no evidence that the plasticisers used in PVC clingfilm are harmful to health, but there is now an alternative material available for microwave cooking which is made from polyethylene film and does not incorporate plasticisers. It is currently available under the brand name Purecling.